THE NOH DRAMA

UNESCO COLLECTION OF REPRESENT-
ATIVE WORKS: JAPANESE SERIES

THE NOH DRAMA

TEN PLAYS FROM THE JAPANESE SELECTED AND TRANSLATED BY THE SPECIAL NOH COMMITTEE, JAPANESE CLASSICS TRANSLATION COMMITTEE, NIPPON GAKUJUTSU SHINKŌKAI

CHARLES E. TUTTLE COMPANY: PUBLISHERS

RUTLAND, VERMONT   TOKYO, JAPAN

NIPPON GAKUJUTSU SHINKŌKAI

(THE JAPAN SOCIETY FOR THE PROMOTION OF SCIENCE)

UNESCO COLLECTION OF REPRESENTATIVE WORKS: JAPANESE SERIES. This work has been accepted in the Japanese Translations Series of the Unesco Collection of Representative Works, jointly sponsored by the United Nations Educational, Scientific and Cultural Organization (Unesco) and the Japanese National Commission for Unesco.

Representatives
Continental Europe: BOXERBOOKS, INC., *Zurich*
British Isles: PRENTICE-HALL INTERNATIONAL, INC., *London*
Australasia: BOOK WISE (AUSTRALIA) PTY. LTD.
104-108 Sussex Street, Sydney 2000

Published by the Charles E. Tuttle Company, Inc., of Rutland, Vermont and Tokyo, Japan, with editorial offices at Suido 1-chome, 2–6, Bunkyo-ku, Tokyo
© 1955, by Nippon Gakujutsu Shinkokai: All rights reserved
Library of Congress Catalog Card No. 60–11007
International Standard Book No. 0-8048-0428-1
First published in 1955 under the title *Japanese Noh Drama: Ten Plays Selected and Translated from the Japanese*
Eleventh printing, 1985

Printed in Japan

CONTENTS

The purpose of all art is to bring sweetness to the hearts of all people and to harmonize high and low.

—ZEAMI MOTOKIYO, *Kwadensho.*

PREFACE

The Japanese Classics Translation Committee appointed in 1934 by the Nippon Gakujutsu Shinkōkai* has for its object the rendering of Japanese classics into foreign languages as a means of acquainting the world with the cultural and spiritual background of Japan. The first enterprise of the Committee was the translation of the *Manyōshū* published in 1940 and reprinted in 1948.

A second enterprise undertaken by the Society is the arduous task of translating the Noh plays which was begun in 1940, soon after the completion of the *Manyōshū*. Since, as in the case of the latter, an adequate and authoritative translation requires the collaboration of a number of scholars and specialists, a Special Committee was formed, consisting of eminent authorities on the subject.

The selection of plays for translation was based upon: 1) intrinsic excellence, 2) cultural and historical significance, and 3) appeal to the Western reader. Fifty plays were chosen for the purpose and rendered into modern Japanese by the Special Committee.

The paraphrases drafted by each member were then submitted to joint sessions of the two Committees for criticism and correction. It was with the aid of these paraphrases that tentative translations were made. These were then revised by English and American scholars and submitted to the Special Committee for examination and revision. The work was continued throughout World War II, although it was not possible for the Committee to meet as often as before. Matters became even worse after the war when many of the members were so engaged with other activities that they were not able to devote much time to this work. Fifty plays have already been translated, but in view of difficult publishing conditions, it has been found impracticable to bring out the whole work at one time and thirty out of the fifty were chosen for publication. The translations were repeatedly subjected to the closest scrutiny, many obscure and difficult passages found in them requiring further research and re-translation.

Fourteen years have elapsed since the initial work was begun, and even now, the Committee is only able to offer as a first instalment ten out of the thirty plays selected.

* The Japan Society for the Promotion of Science.

The Committee desires to acknowledge its deep appreciation for the invaluable help given them by Professors Shigeshi Nishimura and Haxon Ishii who have been responsible for the tentative translations and, in particular, for the painstaking efforts of Professor Arundel del Re who, continuing the work of Messrs. E. H. Pickering, John Morris and Merrill Hitotsuyanagi, has thoroughly revised and is still engaged in revising the dramas selected. But for his ungrudging help the present work of translation could not have been carried through or would have remained incomplete. Thanks are also due to Mr. Sōfū Matsuno for drawing the picture of the Noh stage, to Mr. Motomasa Kanze and the Hinoki Noh Texts Publishing Co. for permission to use the pictures showing the positions of the actors which precede and accompany the texts of the Kwanze school of Noh, both drawn by Mr. Sōfū Matsuno, and to the " Grant in Aid for Publishing Research Result " of the Ministry of Education for providing the funds which made the publication of this work possible.

It is with the deepest regret that the Committee has to record the death of our eminent colleagues, Dr. Seiichi Taki, formerly Chairman of the Committee, and of Dr. Masaharu Anesaki, as well as of Dr. Gen-yoku Kuwaki, Dr. Yoshinori Yoshizawa, Dr. Asaji Nose, and Dr. Toyoichirō Nogami, the last of whom is acknowledged as a great authority on Noh plays, and has written many important works on the subject.

SANKI ICHIKAWA

Chairman of the Japanese Classics Translation Committee of the Nippon Gakujutsu Shinkōkai

Tokyo
April, 1954

GENERAL INTRODUCTION

NOH as an independent and original art form—ultimately destined to supersede the earlier *Dengaku*, *Sarugaku* and other song-dances—incorporates the most significant elements of the former and especially of the *Kusemai* (tune dance). With it a new literary form may be said to have been created. The invention of Noh is attributed to Kwannami Kiyotsugu (1333–1384), a distinguished actor and writer of *Sarugaku* and to his son Zeami Motokiyo (1363–1443), who developed and refined the art under the patronage of Yoshimitsu, the third Ashikaga shogun. In addition to his dramatic activities, Zeami composed a number of works, the most important of which is called the *Kwadensho* (the Book of the Flower), or more properly, *Fūshi-kwadensho* (風姿花傳書) in which he explained the nature and æsthetic principles governing Noh plays, and gave detailed instructions concerning the manner of composition, acting, direction, and production of these dramas.

The term Noh used substantively to denote ' accomplishment,' ' skill,' ' talent,' derives from a verb signifying ' to be able,' ' to have the power,' ' to accomplish something,' and was early applied to actors and dancers. Zeami uses the term to designate that unique type of lyrical drama known as Noh which he subsequently defines as ' elegant imitation.' In the work mentioned above the author stresses that this form of art consists of two fundamental elements—dance and song. In composing a Noh play the poet should, therefore, be careful to select personages from the classics—mythical, legendary or historical—who can appropriately execute songs and dances. He also should always keep the lay-out of the stage in his mind's eye and take care that the action develops naturally out of and expresses the mood created by the music, thus perfectly harmonizing music and acting, singing and dancing. In the light of the above, the Noh drama may, in effect, be described also as a lyrico-dramatic tone-poem in which the text has a function somewhat similar to that of the libretto in a Wagner or Debussy opera. The significance of the action, the beauty of the verse, and the excellence of the music and singing, according to Zeami, are purposely designed to ' open the ear ' of the mind, while the miming (*monomane*) and dancing (*mai*) awaken the emotions of the spectator and ' open his eyes ' to that supreme form of beauty denoted by the word *yūgen*, which is the ultimate goal and the essential element of all æsthetic expression, be it dramatic or lyrical. The term *yūgen* has no exact equivalent in English ; literally it means ' obscure and dark,' but, as used by Zeami, it carries the connotation of half-revealed or suggested beauty, at once elusive and meaningful, tinged with wistful sadness. Zeami and his successors applied *yūgen* as a critical yard-stick not only to works of art but also to the physical appearance and conduct of an individual. Even an old man should, it is said, be presented like a frowning crag with flowers in its crevices.

The accompanying plan, it is hoped, will help the reader the better to visualize the lay-out of the Noh stage and to understand the stage directions accompanying these translations. The stage proper, a square platform of plain white boards, evenly grained, 19 feet 5 inches square, is raised 2 feet 7 inches above the floor of the auditorium (*kenjo*) into which it juts out on three sides. Because of this peculiarity, three fronts are distinguished in the Noh stage : that facing the centre of the auditorium, *shōmen* (front), that facing right, *waki-jōmen* (waki front)—so called because the audience is facing the *waki* when he is sitting on his seat— and that facing left, *jiura* (back of the chorus). The stage is devoid of any decoration or colour except for a large wooden panel (*kagami-ita*) at the back of the stage on which a venerable twisted pine is painted, and a brilliantly coloured curtain screening the entrance to the ' mirror room ' (*kagami-no-ma*) or green room on the extreme left, at the end of the long, covered bridgeway (*hashigakari*) along which the actors approach the stage. To the right of the back stage (*atoza*), in the side-wall between the flute-player's pillar (*fue-bashira*) and the *kagami-ita*, is a small sliding door (*kirido-guchi*) only used by the chorus and stageattendants. The stage is covered by a roof supported at each corner by four square pillars about 15 feet high. A brief flight of steps leads down from it on to a broad strip of shingle called ' white sand bar ' which skirts the base of the stage and the length of the bridgeway. This strip is designed to give the necessary perspective effect to the action taking place on the stage. The bridgeway is flanked, on the auditorium side, by three sapling pines known as ' first ' (nearest the stage), ' second ' and ' third ' pine respectively, each of which serves to mark the position to be taken up by the actors upon their entrance or exit or when the action actually takes place on the bridgeway itself. The chorus sits in an oblong recess on the right of the stage, while the orchestra is situated up-stage— the flute on the right, by the flute-player's pillar, and the drums (large handdrum, small hand-drum and horizontal drum) on his left. On the left of the stage, by the entrance to the bridgeway, is the *shite* pillar (*shite-bashira*) and the *shite* seat, so called because the *shite* or protagonist begins his dance from there.

Behind this, at the back, is the stage-attendants' seat of whom one, called the *kōken* (looker-after), is not only in charge of the stage properties and responsible for seeing that they are laid out and ready for the actors as required, but is the *shite*'s understudy and must be ready to play his part at a moment's notice. The attendants assist the players to change their costumes. Since these changes take place often at the back of the stage in full view of the audience, great quickness and deftness are required in executing them. The corresponding pillar on the right stage goes by the name of *waki* pillar (*waki-bashira*) because by it is the seat of the *waki* or deuteragonist. Opposite, on the left, is the ' eye-fixing pillar ' (*metsuke-bashira*) which serves as a kind of landmark for the actors in taking up their position on the stage which otherwise would be difficult because of their masks. The action proper usually begins and terminates at the *shite* pillar where the protagonist stamps his feet twice to show the play is ended. From the above the importance of the stage lay-out and of its different parts in relation to the action becomes self-evident, no less than its function as the framework for the dance-drama, each phase of which is carefully planned in relation to the fixed stage-positions already mentioned. Hanging under the floor of the stage and the bridgeway are several reverberating jars of earthenware which, acting like a sound-board, serve the purpose of intensifying the stamp of the actor's feet. The position of the jars is indicated in the plan by dotted circles.

The principal actor is called *shite* (performer) who may have one or more attendants (*tsure*), and is supported by the *waki* (bystander) and his one or more attendants (*waki-zure*). Additionally there may be a boy's role (*kokata*) and a walk-on (*tomo*). In typical Noh plays (e.g. *Takasago, Tamura, Tōboku*), the *shite* is, in reality, the only performer, since he alone mimes and dances, the *waki* in the earlier plays being little more than a foil, although in the later ones he becomes the deuteragonist. It will be noticed that in the list of *dramatis personae* the protagonist (*shite*) appears in different guises in the first and the second part. During the interlude (*ai*) [1] designed not only to allow the actor time to change costume but to relieve the tension—the latter purpose presents some interesting analogies with Shakespearean practices—a local worthy, played by the *kyōgen* or comic actor, carries on a semi-humorous dialogue in prose in which he explains the story of the play.

The chorus, while superficially bearing some resemblance to that of Greek tragedy, takes no actual part in the drama itself and wears ordinary costume.

---

[1] This interlude which forms an integral part of the drama should not be confused with satirical farces in prose of the same name, constructed in imitation of the Noh drama.

Its primary role is that of singing the words that accompany the dances executed by the *shite*, but it also comments impersonally upon the events taking place and carries on a dialogue with the *shite* and the *waki*. It consists ordinarily of from eight to ten persons including the leader. As regards the orchestra, it should be noted that the percussion instruments mark the rhythm while the flute provides the melodic theme of the songs and dances. In the present translation the Japanese technical terms for the different types of declamation and singing to be used by the actors or the chorus are given on the left-hand margin of the text. It will be seen that the sung parts alternate with recitatifs, or passages spoken in a declamatory tone. The entrance of the principal actors is generally, though not invariably, preceded by special music which has different names and varies in character according to the kind of singing that follows.

Following the entrance music (*shidai*), the play generally opens with a *shidai* sung by the *waki* alone or in unison with his attendants (*waki-zure*) accompanied by a few notes of the flute and drum taps, subsequently repeated (*jidori*) by the chorus. It is followed by the *michi-yuki* (travel song) also executed by the *waki*. The entrance music of the *shite*, called *issei*, is usually followed by a song of the same name executed by the *shite*. The *sashi* somewhat resembles a recitatif and precedes the songs proper (*uta*) or takes the form of a dialogue as in *Takasago*, I, 4 where it links the *kuri*, a lively piece with varying rhythms, and the *kuse* executed by the chorus except for one verse sung by the *shite*. Yet another form of song is the *rongi* (debate), roughly corresponding to the Greek 'stychomythia,' alternately intoned rather than sung by the chorus and the *shite*. The *machi-utai* (waiting song) chanted by the *waki* and the *waki-zure* to a musical accompaniment, is so called because it announces the appearance of the *shite* in the second part. The *uta* mentioned above are sung by the *shite*, the chorus or the *waki*, and are divided into *age-uta* (high-pitched singing) and *sage-uta* (low-pitched singing). The use of these forms is dictated not only by the text, but by their place in the general musical and rhythmic pattern of the play. To these should be added the *kiri* (finale) sung by the chorus at the end of the play. The spoken portions (*kotoba*) written in prose are classified into *nanori* (name-introducing) delivered by the *waki*, *mondō* (dialogue), and *katari* (narration) delivered in a somewhat monotonous rhythm (*Sanemori*, II, 4).

Dance, mime and rhythm, as already remarked, are distinguishing characteristics of the Noh drama, the ultimate purpose of which is ' significant form ' expressing the aristocratic beauty considered indispensable to ' elegant imitation.' The *mai* (dance), as distinct from the popular *odori*, is a slow dance-sequence that weaves a continuous intricate pattern, the rhythmic movements of which are highly stylized and accompanied by gestures and postures which preserve measure and sobriety even when the tempo becomes livelier and faster, while in the latter which varies so as to express suitably the character and mood of the personage, no attempt is made at realism. The *mai* are of two types : *kakeri* (rush-dance) (*Tamura*, II, 4) and *hataraki* (war-dance) (*Funa-Benkei*, II, 5), which represent battle scenes and in which the dancer mimes rhythmically the narrative sung by the chorus, accompanying it, in the case of *hataraki*, by startling leaps and violent movements, and the *mai* proper which, as a rule, are not sung but concentrate upon beauty of form. To the latter belong the very slow and stately *kami-mai* (god-dance) as in *Takasago*, II, 2 and the *jo-no-mai*, a slow and elegant dance generally assigned to female spirits, such as that performed by Lady Izumi in *Tōboku*, II, 4. The *mai* are in three or five movements, each of which has its particular gestures, steps and postures. The dancer always carries a large fan brilliantly painted and decorated.

In his treatises, Zeami lays particular stress on the vital function of miming in the Noh drama, setting down detailed instructions as to its technique which he illustrates by rough drawings. In these each successive movement and posture of the actor is analyzed and worked out in relation to the character of the personage and to the æsthetic effect to be produced. As conceived by Zeami, the mime might perhaps be compared to a continuous, ever-changing series of rhythmic colour patterns woven by the actor with the aid of gorgeous costumes and masks, the ultimate purpose of which is less to please the eye than to serve as a means of creating the *yūgen* mood which is the very essence of the Noh drama.

While in earlier periods it seemed likely that the costumes tended to follow current fashions, from the Momoyama (1582–1600) to the Genroku period (1688–1703), beauty of colour, line and material rather than historical accuracy were the determining criteria, thus leading to the establishment of very elaborate æsthetic conventions still observed to-day which alone would require a separate treatise. It has been thought desirable and necessary, however, for a better appreciation of the following plays, to include in the stage directions the names and a summary description of the costumes as well as of the wigs and head-gear worn by each person.

As is well known the mask is a distinctive feature of the Noh drama. Unlike classical drama and the *commedia dell'arte*, the Noh as a rule limits the use of the mask to the principal actor and to female characters and aged people. Experts distinguish over one hundred different masks which have been divided into a

number of categories, according to whether they represent divinities or supernatural beings of various kinds, animals, monsters, and men and women old or
young, mad persons and so forth. They are worn with costumes of an appropriate
style and colour. The masks are painted and many of them were designed and
carved by famous artists. Thus in Part Two of *Takasago* the deity of Sumiyoshi
wears a ' man of *Kantan* ' mask created by Tokuwaka (fourteenth century) for
the purpose of portraying a typical noble youth of the Heike clan, and subsequently used for youthful deities performing dances. In Part One of *Tamura*,
the *shite* wears a ' boy' mask and in Part Two, a *Heida* mask representing a
vigorous man in his prime, while Kiyotsune, in the play bearing his name,
wears a ' *chūjō* ' (lieutenant-general) mask, also attributed to the same artist.

As appears from the individual introductions, Noh plays have been classified
into : (1) *Waki* Noh or *Kami* Noh (god plays) because the hero is either a god
or goddess ; (2) *Shura-mono* (Asura plays) whose hero is a famous mediaeval
warrior ; (3) *Kazura-mono* (female-wig plays)—essentially lyrical in character—
in which the protagonist is a woman, whence the name ; (4) Fourth Group
plays, of various types not included either in the preceding or the following
classes, with several important subdivisions such as *Kyōjo-mono* (mad woman pieces),
and *Genzai-mono* (living person pieces) ; and (5) *Kiri* Noh (programme-concluding
plays), auspicious plays having, as a rule, supernatural beings for their protagonists.
As the name indicates, plays to be performed as the last item are chosen from this
group. Each programme, in accordance with prescribed dramatic principles,
should consist of: introduction (*jo*), chosen from among the *Waki* Noh group,
development (*ha*), consisting of three plays one from each of Groups 2, 3
and 4, and climax (*kyū*), invariably a *Kiri* Noh, irrespective of whether
three instead of the customary five plays are to be performed. The *jo-ha-kyū*
principle, as it is called, is also required to be applied to each individual play
and affects the style of the acting as well as the dancing and production. When,
for the sake of variety, it happens that the producer deviates from the above
standard pattern and chooses a *Kiri* Noh instead of a *Waki* Noh as the first piece
on a programme, it is required that the tempo and production of the former
should follow the principle laid down for a *jo* play. Strict adherence to these conventions, while leading to standardization, when skilfully used, gives the programme
artistic unity and produces the desired *yūgen*. The Noh drama, as will be seen in
the plays here translated, is constructed in accordance with the pattern which,
notwithstanding certain minor variations later introduced, was laid down by
Zeami in his treatise entitled *Nōsakusho*. It is divided into two parts ; the first,

serving as a prelude, sets the stage for the drama that will be enacted in the second. Each of these is again divided into scenes that might, in some measure, be compared to the movements of a classical sonata. Unlike what is the case in traditional Western dramatic compositions the scenes are not primarily determined by the entrance or exit of the *dramatis personae*.

The plots of Noh plays are drawn from a variety of Japanese and foreign sources, mythical or legendary, fantastic, historical or contemporary, from the earliest times down to the Muromachi period (1392–1572) ; or inspired by Japanese and Chinese classical poems from the numerous early anthologies. Principal among the former sources are the *Ise Monogatari* (ninth century) and the *Yamato Monogatari* (tenth century), the *Genji Monogatari* (eleventh century), the *Heike Monogatari* (thirteenth century : used for the civil wars between the Heike and Genji clans), the *Kojiki* and the *Nihon Shoki* (both eighth century : used mostly in the *Waki* Noh), and the collection of Indian as well as Chinese and Japanese tales and legends known as the *Konjaku Monogatari* (twelfth century). Apart from its artistic and dramatic significance, the Noh drama, it will be readily appreciated, is of paramount historical interest inasmuch as it reflects, as no other Japanese work does, " the feelings, thoughts, beliefs, superstitions and aspirations and the moral and intellectual life " of the Japanese people during one of the stormiest periods of its history.

The style and language of the Noh drama present considerable linguistic difficulties to anyone not acquainted with classical usage, Buddhist terminology, and the immense body of ancient Chinese and Japanese verse well-known to the highly cultured society of the time, to which frequent allusion is made. In some cases these are quoted in the sung parts, and without such knowledge the significance, and even the meaning, of many passages is inevitably lost. In addition to the literary style full of stylistic affectations in which Zeami required they should be composed, a further difficulty is presented by the *makura-kotoba* (pillow-words), the *kake-kotoba* (pivot-words, i.e. words with a double meaning), the allusive use of certain words, and other conceits which defy the ingenuity of the reader and are the despair of the translator.

The repertories of the principal Noh schools (Kwanze, Komparu, Hōshō, Kongō and Kita) list about 250 plays still being performed, some of which present slight textual variants. The production of the plays also varies to a greater or lesser extent according to the different schools. In the present volume and in those to follow, the text of the Kwanze school is generally followed. Noh play texts known as *utai-bon* (books for *utai*) are published separately or in volumes containing five pieces each but omitting stage-directions and interludes. In-terlinear notes referring to the sung parts provide the user with a rough kind of musical notation, and sometimes small line drawings indicate the positions of the actors in the more important scenes.

In preparing the present translation, the first of a series of volumes, each con-taining ten plays, the Committee has adopted the method previously followed in the *Manyōshū*: after establishing a Japanese text based upon the most recent linguistic studies, it proceeded to make a rough English translation which was then submitted for detailed discussion and revision to a joint committee of Japanese and English scholars. No attempt has been made, however, to reproduce the complex metrical scheme of the original or to do more than present, it is hoped, a faithful yet readable translation, while at the same time preserving as far as possible something of the flavour of the original.

MYŌJIN   "Plucking a spray of plum
           I deck my hair,
CHORUS   And petals, like spring snow, fall o'er my robe."
                                 —Part II, scene 2.

INTRODUCTION

Takasago is a *kami-mai-mono* (god-dance piece) belonging to the *Waki* Noh group which consists of plays of a congratulatory nature performed, as a rule, to celebrate some auspicious occasion. *Takasago* is generally regarded as one of the best examples of this type, by reason of its theme—the legend of the twin pines of Sumiyoshi and Takasago personified by an ancient devoted couple who symbolizes longevity and conjugal fidelity.

The spirit of the Sumiyoshi Pine for countless years crossed sea and mountain to pay a nightly visit to his wife who lived on the coast of the Bay of Takasago in Harima Province, and there held happy converse until the break of day. Although now white-haired, the bond which unites the couple defies time and age, endowing them with eternal vigour and beauty.

While primarily symbolical of longevity and conjugal fidelity, the twin pines also stand for the two great repositories of Japanese poetry, the *Manyōshū*[1] and the *Kokinshū*.[2] According to its traditional role, poetry is one of the main instruments whereby the prosperity and continuity of the state may be ensured. In the present play the happiness and stability of Japan under the Imperial rule is, by implication, attributed to the observance of the high moral and æsthetic principles exemplified in the two anthologies.

While in Part One the aged couple personify the twin pines, in the Interlude the Man of the Place (*kyōgen*) explains that, in effect, they are temporary manifestations of the two deities of Sumiyoshi and Takasago. In Part Two, however, the deity of Sumiyoshi alone appears in his divine form.

At the beginning of the play a Shinto priest and his attendants are on their way by sea from Kyūshū to Miyako and land at the Bay of Takasago in order to visit its famous pine-tree. It is a spring evening and an aged couple are raking up the fallen needles under the pine-tree. At the priest's request they tell him of the ' Twin Pines ' and the reason why they take such care of them. Deeply moved by the tale, the priest decides to visit Sumiyoshi as well, and requests the

---

[1] Eighth century anthology containing 4,516 Japanese poems. A selection of 1,000 pieces was translated into English and published for our Society in 1940 (third impression, 1948).

[2] Tenth century anthology containing 1,100 poems, and the first of a series of twenty-one similar publications subsequently compiled by Imperial order during the following five centuries.

3

Man of the Place to tell him how he can get there. Having embarked on a newly-built boat, he crosses the Inland Sea to Sumiyoshi, where upon arrival he is greeted by the apparition of the noble and youthful-looking deity of the place, and witnesses his performance of a *kami-asobi* (god-play).

Takasago is a typical *Waki* Noh play except for the fact that in this particular play, the *waki* and the *tsure* are represented as a travelling priest and an old woman respectively, instead of as an Imperial messenger or courtier and as a man without a mask, as is usually the case.

When presented on very formal occasions, *Takasago*, like most *Waki* Noh plays, is preceded by *Okina*, in which case the *waki* enters very solemnly. By reason of this special order of performance—'beside' (*waki*) or after *Okina*—*Waki* Noh plays are so called. It may also be performed without *Okina* and is then called *Okina-nashi-no-den* (presentation without *Okina*). Sometimes it is presented after the concluding piece as a *shūgen-no-shiki* (congratulatory offering) at the end of a programme, the first part being then omitted, thus shortening the play to half a Noh (*Han* Noh).

The costumes worn by the aged couple are particularly dignified to suggest the god-like nature of the two personages, and as befits the ceremonial nature of the performance.

Evidence of the popularity of the play throughout the centuries is shown by the fact that it is still customary to chant the famous lines [1] of the chorus in Part One at wedding ceremonies. The aged couple are frequently represented on *kakemono* (hanging scroll) and displayed on special occasions. Porcelain or carved figurines of them, antique as well as modern, are also quite common.

> Author : Zeami Motokiyo (1363–1443)
>
> Source : The Preface to the *Kokinshū* contains a passage stating that the Takasago Pine and the Sumiyoshi Pine are believed to be Twin Pines, while the apparition of the deity of the Sumiyoshi Shrine is suggested by the two poems from the *Ise Monogatari* (Tale of Ise) quoted in Part Two.

---

[1] Calm lies over the Four Seas . . . Under our Sovereign's blessed rule (Part 1, scene 3).

TAKASAGO

Persons

TOMONARI, PRIEST OF THE ASO SHRINE	*Waki*
TWO ATTENDANTS	*Waki-zure*
OLD MAN	*Shite* in Part One
OLD WOMAN	*Tsure*
MAN OF THE PLACE	*Kyōgen*
MYŌJIN, DEITY OF THE SUMIYOSHI SHRINE	*Shite* in Part Two

Place

Takasago in Harima Province (Part One)
Sumiyoshi (or Suminoye) in Settsu Province (Part Two)

Season

Spring

PART ONE

1

While the entrance music shin-no-shidai *is being played,* TOMONARI, PRIEST *of the* ASO SHRINE, *advances to the centre of the stage, followed by* TWO ATTENDANTS, *who take up positions facing* TOMONARI. *The former wears a court minister's cap, heavy silk kimono, lined hunting robe, and white broad divided skirt. The* ATTENDANTS *are also similarly attired.*

TOMONARI and ATTENDANTS
shidai   To-day we don our travelling dress,

5

To-day we don our travelling dress,
Long is the journey before us.

CHORUS   To-day we don our travelling dress,
jidori   Long is the journey before us.

TOMONARI and ATTENDANTS

To-day we don our travelling dress,
To-day we don our travelling dress,
Long is the journey before us.

TOMONARI I am Tomonari, priest of the Aso Shrine in Higo Province in Kyūshū. Never having seen Miyako, I intend to journey thither and shall take the excellent opportunity thus offered me to visit the Bay of Takasago in Harima Province.

TOMONARI and ATTENDANTS

michi-yuki   Clad in travelling attire
To-day we take boat
And set out for distant Miyako,
And set out for distant Miyako.
Soft spring breezes belly our sails;
Gazing ahead and behind,
For days past count
Naught can we see save clouds and sea,
Till what once seemed remote
Now drifts into view
And Takasago Bay is reached at last,
And Takasago Bay is reached at last.

TOMONARI Travelling in haste, we have now reached Takasago. Let us stop here awhile and enquire about this place.

ATTENDANTS As you will, sir.

Moves to the Waki *Seat while the* ATTENDANTS *sit on his right.*

6

2

While the entrance music shin-no-issei *is being
played, the* OLD WOMAN *carrying a besom, followed
by the* OLD MAN *carrying a rake, appears on the
Bridgeway. The* OLD WOMAN *stops by the First
Pine and the* OLD MAN *by the Third Pine. The*
OLD WOMAN *wears an ' old woman' mask, ' old
woman' wig, painted gold-patterned under-kimono,
' not-red' brocade outer-kimono, and broad-sleeved robe;
the* OLD MAN *an ' old man' mask, ' old man' wig,
small-checked under-kimono, and broad-sleeved robe and
white broad divided skirt.*

OLD MAN and OLD WOMAN
issei

The spring breezes
Murmur in the Taka-
sago Pine.
The day is closing in,
And the bell on the hill
Tolls the curfew.

OLD WOMAN The shore mists veil the waves

OLD MAN and OLD WOMAN

That with their voices tell
The sea's ebb and flow.

*Advancing on to the
stage, the* OLD WOM-
AN *stands in the centre
and the* OLD MAN
by the Shite *Pillar.*

OLD MAN   " Who is now left that knew me well?
sashi   This Takasago Pine,
Though venerable indeed,
Is not my old-time friend."[1]

OLD MAN and OLD WOMAN

Countless years have passed
Dropping their snowy mantle on our heads ;

---

[1] Poem by Fujiwara-no-Okikaze (slightly modified) in the *Kokinshū.*

Like aged cranes
On a frosty spring morning
Under the paling moon,
We awake on our rush-mat
To the familiar murmur of the Pine,
And communing with our hearts,
We vent our thoughts in verse.

sage-uta   Our only visitor, the bay-breeze,
Whispers in the Pine ;
From the tree
The needles are falling upon our sleeves ;
Besom in hand,
Let us sweep them away,
Let us sweep them away.

age-uta   Here at Takasago,
Here at Takasago
Each day the Onoye Pine grows older
And advances in years.
How we have aged,
Sweeping away the fallen needles under the
    pine !
Shall we live on for many a year to come
Like the ancient sturdy pines
Of long-famed Iki,[1]
Of long-famed Iki ?

*The OLD MAN
moves to the centre and
and the OLD WOMAN
to the Waki Front.*

3

TOMONARI We have been waiting for a villager. Look, *Rises.*
    an old couple has just appeared over there !
    Pardon me, I have something to ask you.

---

[1] Ancient pine grove on the coast of Chikuzen Province, Kyūshū, alleged according to tradition to have sprung from a spray of pine-needles stuck in the ground by the Empress Jingū (beginning of the third century) while preparing for her expedition against Korea.

OLD MAN   Were you speaking to me? What is it you
   wish?

TOMONARI   Pray tell me which is the Takasago Pine.

OLD MAN   This is the Takasago Pine under which we
   are now sweeping.

TOMONARI   The Takasago and the
   Suminoye Pines are called
   the 'Twin Pines' but how
   can this be when Takasago
   and Sumiyoshi are different
   places?

OLD MAN   You are right. In the Preface to the *Kokinshū*, it is written, "The Pines of Takasago and
   of Suminoye seem like twins." I myself come
   from Sumiyoshi in Settsu Province, but this
   old woman is a native of this place. If you
   know anything about this Pine, you had better   *Turns towards the*
   tell this priest.   OLD WOMAN.

TOMONARI   'Tis passing strange,
   This aged pair should dwell apart,
   He in Suminoye and she in Takasago!
   Tell me, I pray, how this can be.

OLD WOMAN You speak strangely.
   Though miles of land and sea may part
      them,
   The hearts of man and wife are joined by
      love ;
   Naught do they reck of distance.

OLD MAN   Well, you should know!

OLD MAN and OLD WOMAN
   If the Takasago and the Suminoye Pines,
   Though not endowed with feeling,
   Are called the Twins,

How much more then should we—
This woman and myself?
From Sumiyoshi daily I have come
For many years to visit her.
Like these Twin Pines we have grown old
    together
A loving wife and husband.

TOMONARI   Your words fill me with wonder!
But can you not tell me
Some ancient tale about these pines?

OLD MAN   According to the ancient dwellers of this place, they symbolize auspicious Imperial reigns:

OLD WOMAN   Takasago, the old 'Manyōshū' days,

OLD MAN   Sumiyoshi, our present Emperor's[1] reign,

OLD WOMAN   And the unfading greenery of the Pines

OLD MAN   Stands for the art of poetry flourishing as of old,

OLD MAN and OLD WOMAN
    Fostered by the August Majesty whom all revere.

TOMONARI   How noble is your tale!
Now all my doubts have fled.

OLD MAN   Under the warm sunshine, by western seas,

TOMONARI   There at Suminoye,

OLD MAN   Here at Takasago,

TOMONARI   The Pines put on a greener green. . .

OLD MAN   O peaceful days

TOMONARI   Of spring!

CHORUS   Calm lies over the Four Seas,

age-uta   The world's at peace,

While the CHORUS *is singing, the* OLD WOMAN *goes and sits down in front of the* CHORUS.

---

[1] Emperor Daigo (898–930) by whose order the *Kokinshū* was compiled.

The soft wind scarcely mcves the boughs;
In such a reign as this
Happy are the pines born at one time
And growing old together.
In vain words strive to tell
The happiness of those whose days are lived
Under our Sovereign's blessed rule,
Under our Sovereign's blessed rule.

Tomonari sits down.

4

TOMONARI Pray tell me more about the auspicious Taka-
            sago Pine.
CHORUS   Plants and trees, men say, have no soul,
kuri   Yet in due season they blossom and bear
              fruit.
            Under the warm spring sun
            The branches on the south side flower first.
OLD MAN   But the pine-tree
sashi   Throughout the year
            Remains forever unchanged.
CHORUS   Though spring may flee and winter come,
            Its everlasting green
            Even in the snow
            Grows greener.
            " Ten times the pine shall bloom ! "[1]
            So says the ancient prophecy.
OLD MAN   In this auspicious reign
CHORUS   Jewelled words, like glistening dew-drops,

---

[1] Part of a couplet found in the *Shinsen Wakan Rōeishū* (c. 1100), expressing a courtier's wishes for his Imperial master's prosperity. Since, according to an old saying, the pine-tree blossoms once every thousand years, the wished-for length of the reign is ten thousand years—a hyperbolical rhetorical expression frequently found in congratulatory verse and prose of this period.

<table>
<tr><td></td><td>Light up our people's minds,</td></tr>
<tr><td>OLD MAN</td><td>Awaking in all living beings</td></tr>
<tr><td>CHORUS</td><td>The love of poetry.</td></tr>
<tr><td>kuse</td><td>For, as Chōnō writes,[1]</td></tr>
</table>

All nature's voices
Are instinct with poetry.
Herb or tree,
Earth or sand,
Sough of wind and roar of waters,
Each encloses in itself the Universe ;
Spring forests stirring in the eastern wind,
Autumn insects chirping in the dewy grass,
Are they not each a poem?
Yet of all trees the pine is lord
Endued with princely dignity.
Changeless from age to age,
Its fadeless green endures a thousand years ;
And fitly did the Emperor of Shin [2]
Bestow high rank upon the pine ;
In other lands as in our own,
All men unite to praise the pine.

OLD MAN   At Takasago the bell of Onoye is tolling ;[3]   *Rises with the rake in his hand.*

CHORUS   'Tis dawn and freezing hard,

Yet the dark green leaves suffer no harm.

Morning and evening   *The* OLD MAN *mimes the action of raking up the pine-needles.*

The fallen leaves are raked away,

---

[1] Eleventh century poet. The following nine lines are taken from his essay on poetics.

[2] I.e. Ch'in, founder of the Ch'in dynasty (246–207 B.C.). In the twenty-eighth year of his reign he climbed Mt. T'ai in Shantung. While descending the mountains, he was caught in a heavy storm and took shelter under a pine-tree, which miraculously began to grow larger until its branches sheltered the august personage and his retinue from the rain. In recognition of this service the emperor conferred on the tree the fifth court rank.

[3] Poem by Ōe-no-Masafusa in the *Senzaishū* (1187), alluding to the belief that severe frost makes the bell ring of itself.

Yet never fails their store,
But grows more green.
Of all the evergreens
The Twin Pines,—
Blessed emblems of long life—
Have ever been extolled.

The OLD MAN *sits down.*

5

CHORUS   Truly like the pines of ancient fame,
rongi   Truly like the pines of ancient fame,
         Long have you lived. Pray tell me now
         Your past history and your names.

OLD MAN and OLD WOMAN
         Why should we aught conceal?
         We are the spirits
         Of the Twin Pines of Suminoye and Taka-
           sago
         In human form as man and wife.

CHORUS   How marvellous is the miracle
         Of these famed pine-trees!

OLD MAN and OLD WOMAN
         Trees and plants,
         Though not endowed with soul,

CHORUS   —In this auspicious reign,—

OLD MAN and OLD WOMAN
         Nay even the earth and grasses,

CHORUS   Sharing the glory of this realm,
         Live gratefully under our Sovereign's peace-
           ful sway.
         Now to Sumiyoshi I will sail
         And there await your coming.
         —So saying, he boards a fishing-boat

The OLD MAN *rises and mimes the action of boarding a boat.*

13

Moored by the water's edge,
And on a following breeze
Swiftly is wafted out to sea,
Swiftly is wafted out to sea.

The OLD MAN *approaches the* Shite Pillar *and goes out, followed by the* OLD WOMAN.

INTERLUDE

TOMONARI *orders an* ATTENDANT *to call the* MAN OF THE PLACE. *He advances on to the stage from the* Kyōgen *Seat, wearing a check-patterned kimono,* kyōgen *robe and divided skirt. In reply to* TOMONARI'S *question, the* MAN *tells him the legend of the Twin Pines and goes out after offering to take him to Sumiyoshi in his new boat.*

PART TWO

1

TOMONARI and ATTENDANTS

machi-utai   From Takasago Bay,
Hoisting our sails,
Hoisting our sails,
Under the climbing moon
We put out on the flowing tide.
Leaving behind the isle of Awaji[1]
And passing distant Naruo[2]
To Suminoye we have come,
To Suminoye we have come.

Rising, move to the centre of the stage, take up their positions, the former facing the latter.

Return to their seats and sit down.

2

While the entrance music deha *is being played,* MYŌJIN, DEITY OF THE SUMIYOSHI SHRINE *ad-*

[1] Island which separates the Bay of Osaka from the western part of the Inland Sea.
[2] Town at the mouth of the river Muko, east of Kobe.

*vances along the Bridgeway and takes his stand by the
First Pine.   He wears a 'man of* Kantan' *mask,
long black-hair wig, 'open-work' crown, red-and-
white striped heavy silk kimono, lined hunting robe
and white broad divided skirt.*

Myōjin *sashi*	" Long years have sped Since first I saw The Pine of Sumiyoshi by the sea. How many ages has it seen?"[1] " Dost thou not know the bond be- tween us, And how since ancient days My blessings I have poured on the Imperial House?"[2] And, ye musicians of the Shrine, This night let sacred music, Dance and throbs of drums Rejoice my heart!
Chorus	Forth from the waves of the western sea That beat on Aoki-ga-hara,
Myōjin	I first arose—the God himself.[3] 'Tis spring and melting snow Lies lightly on Asaka Beach.[4]
Chorus	By the rocks where men gather seaweed,
Myōjin	" I recline on the ancient pine roots;
Chorus	A thousand years of evergreen fill my palm;

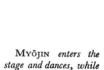

Myōjin *enters the
stage and dances, while
the following lines are
chanted.*

[1] Poem composed, according to the *Ise Monogatari*, by a certain emperor on his visit to the Sumiyoshi Shrine.

[2] Poem composed in reply to the above by the God of Sumiyoshi who appeared assuming a
visible form.

[3] Modified quotation from Urabe-no-Kanenao's poem to the effect that when the God Izanagi
after his visit to the nether world purified himself in the sea at Aoki-ga-hara (Hyūga Province, Kyūshū),
the God of Sumiyoshi was born from the waves.

[4] Name given to the coast near the Sumiyoshi Shrine.

MYŌJIN   Plucking a spray of plum
         I deck my hair,

CHORUS   And petals, like spring snow, fall o'er my
         robe."[1]

MYŌJIN *dances a* kami-mai *dance.*

3

CHORUS   O blessed vision,
rongi   O blessed vision !
         Under the lovely moon
         Before the Sumiyoshi Shrine the God is
         dancing !
         Awe fills our hearts.

MYŌJIN   The voices of the dancing maids rise clear,
         The waters of the bay
         Mirror the Pine of Suminoye—
         This is the ' Blue Sea ' dance.[2]

CHORUS   Straight is the way of the Gods and the
         Sovereign
         And straight the road to Miyako

MYŌJIN   By which the traveller ' Returns to the
         Imperial City.'[3]

CHORUS   Clad in auspicious
MYŌJIN   *Omi* robe—,[4]

CHORUS   Dread spirits quelling, arms are stretched
         out,

---

[1] Quatrain by Tachibana-no-Aritsura contained in the *Wakan Rōeishū* (c. 1013).

[2] I.e. *seigaiha*—a classical dance of Chinese or Korean origin still occasionally performed by the Imperial Household musicians at State banquets.

[3] I.e. *genjō-raku*—a classical dance.

[4] White upper-garment with designs painted green, formerly worn by court dancers and the officiating priest on the occasion of important Shinto rites or at court banquets.

Life and treasure gathering, arms are in-
    wards drawn.
' A Thousand Autumns '[1]
Rejoices the people's hearts ;
And ' Ten Thousand Years '[2]
Endows them with new life.
The soughing of wind in the Twin Pines
With gladness fills each heart,
With gladness fills each heart !

MYŌJIN   *stamps*
twice on the stage at
the Shite *Seat.*

---

[1] I.e. *senshū-raku*—a musical composition by Minamoto no-Yoriyoshi used in 1069 on the occasion
of the *daijōe*, one of the principal Shinto rites connected with the Japanese enthronement ceremony.

[2] I.e. *manzai-raku*—a classical dance attributed to the Empress Wu (623–705) of the T'ang dynasty·

TAMURA

CHORUS   The very sky seems drunk
         With the flowers' beauty.
                    —Part I, scene 4.

INTRODUCTION

Tamura is one of the three *kachi-shura* (victory *Asura*) pieces, the other two being *Yashima* and *Ebira*. Unlike the protagonists of the other *shura-mono* who are generally defeated warriors, the heroes of these plays are victorious generals, thus explaining their great popularity among the samurai in feudal times.

Tamura has three distinctive features. The protagonist, Tamura-maru,[1] was a famous captain who lived before the Gempei (i.e. Genji and Heike) period (1156–1192), instead of being a Genji or Heike warrior, as is usually the case in the *shura-mono*. While the ghosts of defeated warriors, returning to this world, generally lament their sufferings in the world of the *Asura*,[2] here the hero makes no mention of the hell. Finally, the dance-like mime called *kakeri* which in other *shura-mono* describes the ceaseless strife of the *Asura* world, is used in *Tamura* to suggest the exploits of Tamura-maru on the battle-field. In the present play emphasis is laid on the valour of Tamura-maru and his devotion to Kwannon,[3] through whose help he, as commander-in-chief, was enabled to achieve a decisive victory in the campaign against the Eastern barbarians.

Out of gratitude for this victory, Tamura-maru erected the Seisui-ji Temple

[1] Born in the Eastland (see p. 23, note), he early entered the Imperial service, occupying successively with distinction such important posts as general of the Right Wing of the Imperial Body-guard, prefect, commander of an expeditionary army against the barbarians and court minister. His tomb on the outskirts of Kyoto, where he was buried clad in full armour, is called the ' General's Tomb.' It is said that before the outbreak of a war warning rumbles were heard proceeding from his tomb. Upon being appointed to the command of an expeditionary force, it was customary for generals to go and pay homage there.

[2] *Asuras* inhabit one of the six worlds of transmigration. They are full of jealousy and hatred, continuously engaged in fighting one another as a punishment for the deeds of violence committed in their previous life, until they have worked out their *karma* or until, as in the present case, through invocation of Amida and by virtue of His great vow, they have achieved enlightenment and are reborn in the Western Paradise.

[3] Abbreviated form of Kwanzeon Bosatsu, i.e. Bodhisattva hearkening to the prayers of humanity. Kwannon (Skr. Avalokiteshvara) and Seishi (Skr. Mahasthamaprapta), symbolizing respectively mercy and wisdom, are commonly found on either side of Amida in the representation of Amida triad. Whenever Kwannon is invoked by some one in distress, he immediately comes to his succour, assuming a form appropriate to the occasion. It should be noted that in the West Kwannon is usually referred to as the ' Goddess of Mercy,' probably because in the pictorial and sculptural representation the bodhisattva is represented as a female. In India, China and Japan, however, Kwannon, like nearly all other bodhisattvas, are invariably regarded as being of the male sex.

21

(Kiyomizu-dera)[1] in honour of Kwannon on the eastern outskirts of Miyako. Later, a shrine, called Tamura-dō, was dedicated to the memory of the celebrated general in the precincts of the same temple.

It is evening, the cherry-trees are in full bloom and a travelling monk, accompanied by his attendants, is visiting the Seisui-ji Temple. The ghost of Tamura-maru appears to him in the shape of a youth charged with guarding the cherry-trees. In answer to the monk's questions, the lad recounts the history of the temple and after pointing out the famous beauty spots in the neighbourhood, disappears into the Tamura-dō. Filled with pious emotion the monk sits under a cherry-tree and intones the *Lotus Sutra*. The ghost reappears and tells him how with the gracious help of Kwannon he was able to vanquish the demons in the Suzuka Mountains.[2]

While ostensibly centring round Tamura-maru, the play also deals with the founding of the Seisui-ji Temple, thus affording the author an opportunity to extol the boundless mercy of Bodhisattva Kwannon.

The play is divided into two parts, each of which is divided into three conventional sections, i.e. *jo* (introduction), *ha* (development) including *kuse* (song and dance), and *kyū* (climax). In Part One the *kuse* portrays a tranquil landscape in cherry-blossom time; in Part Two it tells how Kwannon aided the warrior Tamura-maru. The contrast in tempo and atmosphere between the two parts is skilfully used to intensify the dramatic effect.

> Author: Zeami Motokiyo (1363–1443)
> Source: *Konjaku Monogatari* (Tales Ancient and Modern)

[1] These two apparently very different names are due to the different ways of pronouncing the Chinese characters used to write the temple's name, i.e. 清水寺, the one being the Chinese and the other the Japanese pronunciation of the original name. The temple belongs to the Hossō sect and is situated on one of the hills on the eastern outskirts of Kyoto. It was founded towards the end of the eighth century by the hermit Genshin. In 798 in fulfilment of his vow, Tamura-maru donated his mansion for the construction of a new temple which was later destroyed by fire and rebuilt. The present buildings date from 1634, when they were completely rebuilt by the Shogun Tokugawa Iemitsu. The precincts contain a shrine called the Tamura-dō dedicated to the general. To the rear of the main edifice there is another shrine at the top of a flight of stone steps, dedicated to Jishu Gongen (Land-Owner Deity), i.e. the *genius loci*. In the ravine, on the edge of which the temple stands, there is a waterfall named Otowa or more descriptively Shiraito (white threads). The flow of water is small, but so clear that it is said to have given the place the name of ' Kiyomizu,' i.e. ' pure water.'

[2] Mountain range separating Ōmi and Ise Provinces which forms the watershed between the east-flowing rivers which pour into the Bay of Ise and the west-flowing ones which empty themselves into Lake Biwa.

TAMURA

Persons

MONK FROM THE EASTLAND [1]	*Waki*
TWO ATTENDANTS	*Waki-zure*
YOUTH	*Shite* in Part One
MAN OF THE PLACE	*Kyōgen*
GHOST OF SAKANOUE-NO-TAMURA-MARU	*Shite* in Part Two

Place

Kiyomizu-dera Temple, Miyako

Season

Spring

PART ONE

1

While the entrance music shidai *is being played, the* MONK FROM THE EASTLAND, *accompanied by* TWO ATTENDANTS, *crosses the Bridgeway and goes to the centre of the stage. He wears a pointed hood, plain kimono, and broad-sleeved robe. The* ATTENDANTS *are also similarly attired.*

MONK and ATTENDANTS

shidai   Across many a province following the Imperial highway,

Across many a province following the Imperial highway,

---

[1] Literal translation of Tōgoku, the comprehensive name given to the provinces east of Kyoto, including the Tōkaidō.

We hasten towards spring-clad Miyako of the nine-gates.[1]

CHORUS
jidori

Across many a province following the Imperial highway,

We hasten towards spring-clad Miyako of the nine gates.

MONK   I am a monk from the Eastland. As I have not yet seen Miyako, I am journeying thither in spring-time.

MONK and ATTENDANTS
michi-yuki

'Tis mid-March,

Across the tranquil sky,

Across the tranquil sky

Leisurely rolls the sun,

And yonder swathed in mist lies Otowa Hill.

At last, where crystal waters softly murmur,

We reach Kiyomizu-dera,

We reach Kiyomizu-dera.

MONK   Travelling in haste, we have reached a temple in Miyako which people call the Seisui-ji. Here the cherry-trees are in full bloom. Let us wait till some one passes by and ask him about this place.

FIRST ATTENDANT

It will be well to do so.

They cross to the Waki Seat and sit down.

2

While the entrance music issei *is being played, the*

---

[1] Conventional epithet for the Imperial City. The phrase was borrowed from ancient China, where visitors from abroad to the Imperial court had to pass through nine gates, the first of which being situated on the frontier.

YOUTH *enters the stage carrying a* hagi *besom*[1] *in his hand and takes his stand by the* Shite *Pillar. He wears a ' boy ' mask, flowing black-hair wig, brocade head-band, embroidered kimono and broad-sleeved robe.*

YOUTH	The cherry-blossoms
issei	In the precincts of the shrine
	Are Spring's offering to the Deity.[2]
sashi	Many a place is famed for cherry-trees,
	But none can boast such blossoms ;
	Methinks the charity of Kwannon
	Adds lustre to their hue.
	Like fragrance of spring flowers,
	His boundless love and mercy
	Fill the land of the Ten Evils[3]
	And like the autumn moon,
	His thirty-three-fold form[4]
	Upon the waters of the Five Defilements[5]
	Shines undefiled.
sage-uta	See ! The garden of the God
	Is filled with snow !
age-uta	In dazzling white
	Buried are clouds and mist,

[1] Broom made of bush-clover stems.

[2] I.e. Jishu Gongen. See p. 22, note 1.

[3] Ten sins warned against in the Buddhist Ten Commandments, i.e. murder, theft, adultery, lying, immoral language, equivocation, slandering, covetousness, anger, wrong ideas, the first three being committed by the body, the middle four by the tongue, and the last three by the mind.

[4] It is said in the twenty-fifth chapter of the *Lotus Sutra*, which describes the all-embracing merciful powers of Bodhisattva Kwannon, that, whenever appealed to, he immediately comes to the rescue of the distressed, taking one of his thirty-three visible forms.

[5] Or Five Corruptions. The world during and since Sakyamuni's time is characterized by five evil conditions, i.e. corruption of the times (abundance of calamities), corruption of thought (prevalence of wrong ideas), corruption of feeling (evil passions), corruption of people (weak bodies and degenerate characters), corruption of life (man's life shortened).

Buried are clouds and mist.
Try as I may, no branches can I see ;
Double and single blossoms hang like clouds
Over Miyako of the nine-gates,
Set in the frame of hills
Decked in their spring glory,
Decked in their spring glory.

3

MONK	Hullo, boy, I want to ask you a question.	*Rises and addresses the* YOUTH.

YOUTH   Were you speaking to me, sir? What can
I do for you?

MONK   I see, you are sweeping beneath the trees
with a jewelled besom. Are you perhaps the
gardener?

YOUTH   Yes, I minister to the deity
of the place. I always sweep
beneath the trees at blossom-
time, so I may be called the
gardener or servant of the
shrine. Anyhow you may
consider me belonging to the
shrine.

MONK   Since you seem to be so closely connected
with this shrine, will you tell me the history
of the temple?

YOUTH   You must know that this
katari 'Seisui-ji' Temple was founded in the second year of
Daidō[1] by Sakanoue-no-Tamura-maru in fulfilment of
his vow. Long ago, at the

[1] I.e. A.D. 804.

Koshima Temple, in Yamato Province, there lived a monk called Genshin, who resolved to see Kwannon in human form. One day seeing a golden light proceeding from the upper reaches of the River Kotsu,[1] he followed it to its source. There he found an old man, who said to him, " I am Gyōe Koji. You will meet with a benefactor and with his aid you will build a great temple in my honour." With that the old man flew away towards the east. Now Gyōe Koji was no other than a manifestation of Bodhisattva Kwannon in human shape.

The donor he was told to wait for
Proved to be Tamura-maru.

CHORUS
age-uta

Since then
The fame of this Pure Water[2]
Has never ceased.
Diverse are the God's great vows
And countless as his thousand hands.[3]
All praise to His Great Charity !
His blessed vows reach every corner of the
    land
And multitudes of men.
From the Land of Supreme Bliss
Kwannon visits this world of sorrow
To heal our ills.
Should we not then adore him with all our
    being,

The YOUTH *goes to the* Metsuke *Pillar.*

Approaching the Shite

---

[1] River which springs in Mie Prefecture and flows into the river Yodo below Kyoto.

[2] I.e. Kiyomizu.

[3] The Thousand-armed Kwannon enshrined in the temple has actually only forty arms, the hands of which have an eye in the middle of each palm. This form of Kwannon symbolizes the immeasurable powers and unlimited devices which the bodhisattva uses to save those who rely upon him.

Should we not then adore him with all our being?

Pillar, the YOUTH *hands his besom to a Stage-attendant.*

4

MONK — Well, it is rare nowadays to find a person as interesting as yourself. I suppose all the places I can see from here are famous. Please tell me about them.

YOUTH — Yes, they all are famous. Ask me any question you like and I will tell you with pleasure.

MONK — First, tell me what is that pagoda to the south?

Faces the Front audience.

YOUTH — That is the Seigan-ji Temple[1] of Uta-no-nakayama. You can also see as far as Ima-gumano.[2]

Faces the Front audience.

MONK — What is that temple to the north, whose evening bell is now tolling?

Turns towards the Flute-player and looks upwards.

YOUTH — It is the sacred 'Vulture Peak' Temple.[3] But see! The moon is rising over Otowa Hill and shines upon the cherry-blossoms round the Jishu Gongen. This is the finest view.

Looks in the same direction and then turns towards the Waki Pillar.

The YOUTH *and the* MONK *again face the Front audience.*

MONK — This is Spring's rapturous hour,
Which banishes all other thoughts.

---

[1] Famous temple situated to the southeast of Kiyomizu among the same hills which was first established in the ninth century and is now partly in ruins.

[2] Shinto shrine, farther south, established in the twelfth century by an ex-emperor who was a devotee of the goddess Izanami enshrined at Kumano. Wishing to have another shrine to the goddess near Miyako, he built the present one. Hence the name " Ima-Gumano " (i.e. Now-Kumano).

[3] Washino-o in Japanese. In China and Japan a temple, as a rule, has two names, that of the mountain and that of the temple itself. In the present case the former is ' Vulture Peak ' and the latter Shōbō-ji. Dengyō Daishi, the founder of the Japanese Tendai sect, founded the temple towards the end of the eighth century soon after his return from China, giving it this name because the shape of the hill, on which it is situated, resembled that of the Vulture Peak in India, on which Buddha preached the *Lotus Sutra.*

YOUTH   Truly we should cherish it jealously.

MONK   We should indeed.

MONK and YOUTH

" The scent of flowers,
A hazy moon,
A single spring evening
Are worth a thousand golden pieces." [1]

YOUTH   Nay, far more precious
Than a thousand coins of gold
Is this very hour.

The YOUTH *touches him on the shoulder.*

CHORUS   The cherry-blossoms of the Jishu
sage-uta   Gongen !
What a breath-taking sight !
The moon-rays pierce the branches,
Evening breezes tempt the blossoms,
Filling the air with snowy petals
And ravishing the heart !

The MONK *goes to the* Waki *Seat and sits down. The* YOUTH *dances while the following lines are chanted.*

kuse   Truly worthy of its name
Is Flowery Miyako under the vernal sky,
When spring is decked in all her beauty.
Endless delight
Are the green shadows of the budding willows
Stirred by the gentle breezes,
Like the silvery threads which ceaseless flow
Over the Otowa waterfalls !
Matchless in hue
The cherry-blossoms of the Jishu Gongen !

YOUTH   " Have but faith in me,

[1] Quoted from a poem by Su Tung-po (蘇東坡) (1036–1101) which may be rendered :
    A single hour of a spring evening is worth one thousand
      pieces of gold ;
    Flowers send forth scent and the moon is misty ;
    The notes of the flute from the upper storey grow faint ;
    The swing in the court hangs motionless in the night air.

CHORUS

Ye, who are like moxa-weeds on Shimeji
    Moor:
While yet in this world I dwell."[1]
This vow shall ever inviolate endure
Like the ' Pure Water' of Kiyomizu;
And as they deck the willow-trees with
    tender green,
So does His virtue make dead boughs to
    bloom.
In the pale moonlight,
Cherry-trees everywhere are in their glory;
The very sky seems drunk
With the flowers' beauty.
O magic springtide,
O magic springtide !

The YOUTH *sits
down in the centre of
the stage.*

5

The MONK *turns to-
wards the* YOUTH.

CHORUS
rongi

From your noble looks
You seem no common mortal.
What may your name be?

YOUTH

Though I be nameless,
If you would learn who I am,
Watch as to the temple I return.

CHORUS

Where is your home? Is it as close
As are lacèd reeds in a wattle fence,
" Or far from here

YOUTH

Lost among the pathless mountains?"[2]

---

[1] Poem in the *Shin Kokinshū* (1205) attributed to the Kiyomizu Kwannon. It is supposed to have been addressed to a woman in grief who said that if there was no hope, she would take her own life.

[2] Quoted from an anonymous poem in the *Kokinshū* which reads:

    Lost among the mountains
    With no sign of any village far or near,
    'Tis sad to hear
    The cuckoo's cries.

CHORUS

> If you are in doubt,
> Watch where I go—so saying,
> He leaves the Jishu Gongen.
> Look, he seems moving down the hill,
> No, he's climbing upwards
> To where Tamura Shrine tops the slope,
> And throwing wide its moon-blanched
> portals,
> He glides across the hall
> And vanishes into the sanctuary.

The YOUTH *rises and takes a few steps forward and then moves away from the* Metsuke *Pillar towards the* Orchestra *and with his fan he mimes the action of opening the door and then steps up to the* Shite *Pillar and goes out.*

INTERLUDE

The MAN OF THE PLACE *who has been sitting on the* Kyōgen *Seat rises and enters the stage. He wears a check-patterned kimono,* kyōgen *robe and divided skirt. In answer to the* MONK'S *enquiry as to who was the mysterious figure which has just disappeared into the sanctuary, the* MAN *replies that it must have been the* GHOST OF Tamura-maru *himself and suggests that he would do well to stay awhile and recite the* Lotus Sutra *for him. Approaching the* Waki *Seat, he addresses the* MONK, *and relates the history of the temple and how* Tamura-maru *routed the demons of the* Suzuka *Mountains.*

PART TWO

1

MONK and ATTENDANTS

machi-utai

> All through the night
> Under a rain of petals,
> Under a rain of petals,
> As the moon takes her unfaltering way,

Seated in the Courts of the Holy Law
Canopied with wondrous flowers,
We chant the Holy Sutra,
We chant the Holy Sutra.

2

While the entrance music issei *is being played, the*
Ghost OF TAMURA-MARU *enters the stage and takes*
his stand by the Shite *Pillar. He wears a* Heida
mask, long black-hair wig, tall black cap secured by a
white head-band, heavy silk kimono, gold-brocade robe
with left shoulder uncovered, divided skirt and sword.

Turns towards the
MONK.

TAMURA-MARU
sashi

By Kiyomizu-dera's waterfall
I shall address this traveller,

Faces the Front
audience.

Whom from a past life
I was ordained to meet,
Perhaps because we both
Once drank of the same stream.[1]
His night-long chanting of the Sutra
Commends my soul to the protection
Of Kwannon the All-Merciful.

MONK

O wondrous sight !
Behold ! A human form
Gleaming amidst the flowers !
Who may you be ?

TAMURA-MARU

No longer shall I conceal my name ;
Sakanoue-no-Tamura-maru am I

---

[1] Allusion to a proverbial saying commonly met with in mediaeval Japanese literature. In its
complete form it runs : " If two people happen to rest under the same tree or to drink from the same
stream, this apparent accident was destined to occur because of some relationship existing between them
in a former life." The idea is Buddhistic.

Who lived in the reign of Heizei,[1]

Fifty-first Emperor.

CHORUS 'Twas I subdued the barbarous Eastern tribe

And vanquished the demon hosts;

I proved myself a loyal warrior

And brought peace back to the Imperial
realm.

All this was wrought

By virtue of Holy Sattva

Who dwells within this temple.

3

CHORUS An order from the gracious Sovereign

sashi Decrees I shall subdue

The tribe of demons

Infesting the Suzuka Mountains

And restore peace to town and country.

Obeying his command I raised an army.

Hither came I on the eve of departure;

And calling on All-Merciful Kwannon

I made my vow.

TAMURA-MARU *goes
to the centre of the stage.*

TAMURA-MARU *sit
on a stool.*

TAMURA-MARU

Marvellous signs were granted;

CHORUS The Image smiled.

Confidently we set forth against the evil
tribe—

kuse "On the broad earth, under the vast
heavens

Can there be a land our Sovereign ruleth
not?"—[2]

---

[1] Reigned 806–809. Tamura-maru also served the preceding Emperor Kammu (781–806).

[2] Poem in the *Shi-King* (Book of Odes). Literally translated, the lines run:

> Under the all-covering heavens
> Or as far as the shores of the continuous land,
> There is not a foot of land that is not the king's,
> Nor a man who is not his subject.

Anon we crossed Ōsaka Pass[1]
Whose barrier-gates no longer shall be
    closed.
Leaving Awazu Wood
Hard by the rippling lake,
We reached the Stony Mountain Temple.[2]
Here we invoked the Sattva enshrined at
    Kiyomizu ;
Then following the Ōmi Road,
Clattered across the Long Bridge of Seta,
Steeds prancing with warlike ardour.

Stamps on the stage to indicate the clatter of horses' hoofs.

TAMURA-MARU

The hills of Ise now come near.

Rises.

CHORUS

Like eager plum-trees bursting into bloom,
The stalwart warriors forward press,
Each with other vying
Like springtime flowers and autumn leaves.
This land divine—
O'er its soil and trees our Sovereign
    rules,—
As long as Kwannon's promise aids us,
Is guarded by gods and countless buddhas.
Unmindful of my warriors' approach,
Like unsuspecting deer
The demons lie on Suzuka,
A place of holy memories,
For in ancient days

Going to the front of the stage, TAMURA-MARU dances while the following lines are chanted.

---

[1] Pass running across the boundary line between the metropolitan province of Yamashiro and Ōmi Province. In olden times it was marked by a barrier which was strictly guarded. The phrase qualifying Ōsaka Pass expresses the desire for perfect peace throughout the land.
[2] I.e. Ishiyama-dera. The temple stands on the right bank of the river Seta issuing from Lake Biwa. Founded in the eighth century, its main edifice has remained intact. The temple is dedicated to Kwannon. According to tradition, it was in one of the chambers of this temple that Lady Murasaki wrote her great work the *Genji Monogatari*.

The Suzuka purification[1] was here performed.

4

CHORUS   Hill-shaking and stream-tossing demon-cries
Fill the earth and echo to the skies,
And the green hills tremble before our eyes.

A kakeri, suggestive of TAMURA-MARU'S *encounter with the demons, is executed.*

5

TAMURA-MARU

    Ye demons, hearken to my words: Remem-
ber what happened in ancient times when the
demons serving the Rebel Chikata were scattered by Heaven for their defiance of the
Imperial will; and hardly had they left their
leader, when the traitor was vanquished.[2]
    How dare you therefore haunt
The Suzuka Mountains hard by Miyako?

CHORUS   In the far distance lies the Ise Sea,
In the far distance lies the Ise Sea.

*During the whole of
the concluding scene,*
TAMURA-MARU *ac-
companies the words by
dramatic gestures and
movements.*

*Goes towards the
Flute-player*

[1] In ancient times an Imperial princess newly appointed to serve as priestess of the Ise Shrine used to undergo purification in the waters of the river Suzuka.

[2] Anecdote found in the *Taiheiki* where it reads as follows: In the reign of the Emperor Tenji a wicked man called Fujiwara-no-Chikata with four demons in his service, called respectively Metal, Wind, Water and Invisible Demon, endowed with various superhuman powers, succeeded in alienating the people of Ise and Iga Provinces from the Imperial rule. Consequently a courtier-warrior Ki-no-Tomo-o was sent to subdue the rebels, and having arrived in the enemy territory, sent the demons this poem:

> Since all the land,
> Even the trees and grasses,
> Belong to our gracious Sovereign,
> What place is there for demons to live in?

On reading this, the demons were terrified lest they should be punished by Heaven for serving a wicked man in defiance of a merciful legitimate prince, and at once fled the country. Thus deserted, Chikata was soon vanquished.

Along the shore,
Numberless as the pines of Ano[1]
Swarm the demon-hosts
Who spew forth inky clouds and dreadful
    thunderbolts,
Then, transformed into countless
    ranks of horse,
Like mountains upon us they bear down.

TAMURA-MARU

    See yonder—a miracle, miracle!

CHORUS   See yonder—a miracle, miracle!
Above the banners of our host
The dazzling rays of the Thousand-Armed
Flash across the sky;
Each arm holds a mercy-bow,
And each its wisdom-arrow;
Together a thousand arrows He lets fly
Which beat like rain or hail upon the
    demons
Till all are stricken down.
Praise be to Kwannon! Praise be to
    Kwannon!
" With Whose aid,
Ever to be invoked[2]
Against all evil spells and poisons,
Our foes we vanquished.
Thus wickedness
Is turned by Him against its authors,
Is turned by Him against its authors."

TAMURA-MARU
*stamps twice on the
stage at the* Shite *Seat.*

Such, indeed, is Kwannon's divine power.

[1] Famous pine grove on the Bay of Ise near the city of Tsu which was wiped out by an earthquake in the fifteenth century.

[2] Quoted from the Kwannon chapter of the *Lotus Sutra.* A more literal translation of the Chinese version would be: " When, imperilled by spells or poisons a person invokes the saving power of Kwannon, he shall find these evils falling back on to the head of the evil-doer."

SANEMORI

OLD MAN   What if my feeble legs move slow;
Like Paradise,
The temple is "not far from here!"
Namu Amida Butsu!
—Part I, scene 3.

INTRODUCTION

Sanemori, like *Tamura*, belongs to the group of *Asura* plays, but departs from most of them in having an old man for its hero.

Saitō-Bettō-Sanemori, who belonged to the Fujiwara clan and was descended from illustrious ancestry, was born in Echizen Province (A.D. 1111). At first he sided with the Genji, but later, went over to the Heike and became one of their famous military leaders. He served Taira-no-Koremori, Commander of the Heike army, which was opposing the advance of Minamoto-no-Yoshinaka,[1] and was defeated and killed at Shinowara [2] in Kaga Province at the age of seventy-two. Before setting out to battle, having a premonition that he would not return alive, Sanemori requested and obtained from Munemori, chief of the Heike clan, the privilege of wearing a red-brocade robe granted only to generals. Another circumstance which has made his last fight famous was that he dyed his grey hair raven-black in order to look youthful. Though in skill, agility and bravery he rivalled the younger warriors, he was finally unhorsed by his opponent, who cut off his head.

Although two centuries have passed since his death on the battle-field of Shinowara when the play opens, the spirit of Sanemori is still unsaved and haunts the battle-field where he tried in vain to engage in single combat with Lord Kiso, the enemy commander-in-chief. A travelling Buddhist priest—Yugyō

---

[1] Born in 1154 and dying in 1184, he was a cousin-german of Yoritomo, first shogun of Japan. His father (Yoshikata) was killed when he was two years old. At that time Yoritomo, taking pity on the orphan, had him secretly conveyed to the house of his nurse in the Kiso Mountains in Shinano Province where he was brought up, on account of which he came to be known as Kiso Yoshinaka. In 1180 in answer to Prince Mochihito's request that the Genji should attack the Heike, Yoshinaka rallied together the local Genji troops, while Yoritomo did the same in the Tōkaidō provinces. Rapidly increasing in numbers both armies converged on Miyako, one advancing along the Japan Sea, the other along the Pacific coast. After dealing the enemy a crushing defeat, Yoshinaka entered Miyako, which had been hastily evacuated by the Heike. The victory soon stirred up bitter rivalry between the two Genji generals and finally led to open war. The battle in which Sanemori lost his life took place during Yoshinaka's advance on Miyako.

[2] Village in Kaga Province, adjoining Sanemori's native province, Echizen, both situated on the Japan Sea.

Shōnin [1]—who is passing through the district, happens to visit Shinowara, where he spends some days preaching and praying with the villagers. Attracted by the chanting of prayers, Sanemori appears in the shape of an old rustic who listens in rapt attention to the priest's sermons. Noticing him, the priest asks him who he is and having learned his story, performs special rites for the repose of Sanemori's tormented spirit by virtue of which he is able at last to be reborn in the Western Paradise.

In this play, the author deftly links up the hero's tale of the battle (*katari*) and the episode of the red-brocade robe (*kuse*), with the circumstantial narrative of his attempted attack on Lord Kiso and his death at the hands of a follower of the latter (*rongi*).

The chief merit of the play lies in the beauty of the speeches delivered by the majestic white-haired Sanemori, to the accompaniment of appropriate singing and dancing. At the same time they possess an inner significance in that they form part of the warrior's confession, without which he cannot experience the spiritual conversion required before he can reap the fruits of Amida Buddha's great vow: " Let Amida's name be once invoked and unfathomed sin shall melt away." [2]

> Author : Zeami Motokiyo (1363–1443)
>
> Source : *Heike Monogatari* (Tale of the Heike) and contemporary local traditions.

---

[1] Priest of the Ji sect of Jōdo-kyō (Pure Land Buddhism), founded by Ippen Shōnin in 1272. The Yugyō Shōnin in question was the fourteenth head of the sect. The name, meaning ' travelling priest,' is the common title given to the chief priest of the sect because his main duty is to travel continuously all over the country, propagating the tenets of the sect. Taami, the other name mentioned in the *dramatis personae,* is also a title assumed by successive heads of the sect. The present priest's proper name is not given.

[2] See p. 51, note 1.

SANEMORI

Persons

PRIEST (THE VERY REVEREND TAAMI YUGYŌ SHNŌIN)	*Waki*
TWO ATTENDANTS	*Waki-zure*
MAN OF THE PLACE	*Kyōgen*
OLD MAN	*Shite* in Part One
GHOST OF SAITŌ-BETTŌ-SANEMORI	*Shite* in Part Two

Place

Shinowara, Kaga Province

Season

Summer

PART ONE

1

The PRIEST, *followed by* TWO ATTENDANTS, *appears and crosses the Bridgeway. They wear pointed hoods, small-checked under-kimonos, broad-sleeved robes, and white broad divided skirts. Advancing on to the* Waki *Seat, the* PRIEST *sits on a stool, while the* ATTENDANTS *sit on the floor beside him. After a short interval, the* MAN OF THE PLACE *enters and stands by the* Shite *Pillar. He wears a check-patterned kimono, sleeveless robe and trailing divided skirt.*

41

MAN OF THE PLACE

    The person who is speaking is an inhabitant of Shinowara. Now the Very Reverend Taami Yugyō Shōnin XIV is staying here and delivering moving sermons to grateful multitudes. About noon he begins to commune aloud with himself each day to the wonderment of the people, who variously comment among themselves upon his strange behaviour. Since it is my duty to wait upon this holy man, I have been asked to request him to explain it. To-day, shortly after noon, I shall go to him and make bold to question him. If any of you happen to hear him talking to himself, please let me know. Let this be clearly understood !

Turns and goes to the Kyōgen Seat.

2

PRIEST	Beyond ten billion Buddha-lands [1]
sashi	Lies Amida's Western Paradise ;
	Long is the way a ghost must tread
	Ere it may be reborn therein.
	Yet if Amida dwell within our hearts,
	This very place is Paradise.
	Voices of prayer arise
	From folk of high and low degree.
ATTENDANTS	Day after day, both morn and eve,
	Crowds flock to listen to the Law :
PRIEST	Truly, who is there whom Buddha's Vow
ATTENDANTS	Of Universal Salvation
PRIEST	Does not embrace ?

PRIEST and ATTENDANTS

age-uta   " Within himself,

---

[1] The *Amitabha Sutra* (smaller Sukhavatu vyuha) opens with the words, " Westward from here, beyond ten billion Buddha-lands, there is a world called the ' Highest Happiness.' "

Upon Amida's name each one will ponder,
Upon Amida's name each one will ponder,
When he departs from the Place of Law."[1]
In Amida's net
Caught are both wise and foolish.
Upon the boat of Buddha's Law,
Wise and foolish, all would I bear
Unto the shores of that Blessed Land.
This is the " Easy Way,"[2]
This is the " Easy Way."

3

While the foregoing lines are being chanted, the
OLD MAN *appears and advances along the Bridge-*
way to the First Pine. He wears a ' smiling old
man' mask, ' old man' wig, plain kimono and
broad-sleeved robe.

OLD MAN   " Bathed in the glory of the westering
sashi   sun,
Voices of angel-pipes
Float from yon solitary cloud,
Which bears the heavenly host
To welcome the departing soul."[3]
O blessed vision ! A purple cloud
To-day again hovers above this place.

Turns towards the stage and joins his hands in prayer.

---

[1] Quoted from a poem by Ippen Shōnin.

[2] As opposed to the " hard way " through self-discipline and good works preached by other Buddhistic sects. The " easy way," taught by Jōdo-kyō, only requires absolute faith in Amida and repeated invocation (*nembutsu*) of his name, by virtue of which the believer after death is received into the Western Paradise where, seated on a Lotus-Seat in the Lake of Treasure (see p. 50, note 1) he will finally attain Buddhahood by listening to his teachings.

[3] Verse composed by the monk Jakushō (tenth–eleventh c.) just before he died. After serving for a time as prefect of Mikawa Province, he later renounced the world and entered a Buddhist monastery on Mt. Hiei in order to devote himself to Buddhist study and exercises. He subsequently went to China where his learning and virtue aroused the admiration and respect of the Sung emperor. He died at Hangchow at the age of seventy-three.

I hear the sound of gongs and prayers; the sermon will soon begin. I am so age-worn that my limbs ache whether I sit or stand. Though I am too feeble to enter the temple, at least I can stand outside and listen to the sermon as best I may.

Though Amida's saving vow shines dazzl-
  ingly
On him who once invokes his name,
I cannot yet perceive
The glory of the Law,
My eyes being dim with age.
What if my feeble legs move slow;
Like Paradise,
The temple is " not far from here !" [1]
Namu Amida Butsu !

Entering the stage, and sitting down by the Shite *Pillar and turning towards the* PRIEST, *joins his hands in prayer.*

4

PRIEST   Come now, old man ! You are never absent from the daily service ; I can see you are a devout believer. But as others cannot see you, they wonder to whom I am speaking and what I am saying. Please tell me your name to-day.

OLD MAN   Your request is most unexpected. I am a yokel living in this remote corner of the land ; if I were a person of any importance, I would tell you my name. Since your holiness's coming to this place, it seems to me as if

[1] In the *Kwan Muryōju-kyō* (*Amitayurdhyana* : Sutra of the Meditation on the Buddha of Ever-lasting Life) it is written, " Then the Universally Reverend (Sakyamuni) says to Queen Videhi, ' Dost thou know that Amida is not far from here ? ' "

Buddha himself had come to save my soul,
and I say to myself,

> A lucky man indeed am I
> To have seen this age
> In which the ' Invocation of the Name ' is
> taught.

> Like the eyeless turtle [1]
> Who alights at sea upon a floating plank,
> Or like the lucky man
> Who sees the *udambara* [2] burst into bloom,
> My bliss is greater than my years can bear,
> And tears of joy drench these sleeves.
> Filled with joy unspeakable
> That, now, even this man
> May hope to be reborn in Paradise,
> Am I loath again to utter
> The name I once bore
> In this world of attachment and trans-
> migration.

PRIEST   Indeed, what you say is very reasonable ;
yet revealing who you are may, in truth, lead
you to confess and be converted. Now without
more ado tell me your name.

OLD MAN   Must I then reveal my name?

PRIEST   Indeed you must. Do so at once.

OLD MAN   Pray bid the others leave your presence, and
I shall then draw near you and tell you who
I am.

---

[1] According to a Buddhist parable there is in a wide ocean a turtle which has no eye in its head but one in its belly and a floating plank with a hole through it. If the blind turtle should happen to find the plank, attach itself to the underside, and apply its belly-eye to the hole, he could see the sun in heaven. The parable is used to illustrate how rare it is for an unenlightened soul to learn about Buddhism.

[2] Mythical plant supposed to flower for a thousand years but to take a thousand years to come into bud and another thousand years before the flower opens. The flowering of the *udambara* is used as a parable illustrative of the truth expressed in the preceding parable.

PRIEST   They cannot see your shape, but, if you wish, I'll have them leave me. Draw closer and speak your name.

OLD MAN   As you must have heard tell, many years ago Saitō-Bettō-Sanemori of Nagai[1] was killed in battle here at Shinowara.

Approaches the centre of the stage and sits on the floor.

PRIEST   I know he was a warrior of the Heike clan, a famous captain. But at present I do not want to hear the tale of the battle. Just tell me your name.

OLD MAN   Wait! You will soon see why. It is said that the locks and beard of Sanemori's severed head were washed in the pond before you. Perhaps because his spirit still clings to this place, the folk hereabouts say they sometimes see him haunting it like a ghost.

PRIEST   What? You mean his ghost still appears?

OLD MAN   " The cherry-tree mingling with other trees
        upon the mountain-side
Betrays itself at flowering time."[2]
So 'tis with this old tree.

PRIEST   How wonderful!
Methought I was listening
  to the ancient tale of
  Sanemori,
But now indeed, I see
'Twas yours.

Are you then the very ghost of Sanemori?

OLD MAN   Yes, I am Sanemori's ghost. While the ethereal part of my soul is in the world of

---

[1] Village in Musashi Province near the present Asakusa. Sanemori lived there while serving the Genji family.
[2] Poem by Minamoto-no-Yorimasa, a famous Genji general, included in the *Shikashū* (1153).

	gloom, the sensuous part lingers on earth,[1]
PRIEST	And in this world of bondage
OLD MAN	Has lived more than two hundred years,
PRIEST	But still remains unsaved.
	As Shinowara Pond
OLD MAN	Day and night is stirred by ceaseless ripples,
PRIEST	So the darkened soul
OLD MAN	Is tossed by thoughts
PRIEST	'Twixt dream
OLD MAN	And waking.
age-uta	Like hoar-frost on the withered grass
	My locks and beard are white with age,
CHORUS	" My locks and beard are white with age,
	And since this shape is temporarily assumed,
	I would not others see them,
	Nor that my name be noised abroad,
	Lest rumour's tongue again put me to shame "—
	Thus leaving the holy presence,
	He moves away, but as he nears
	The pond of Shinowara
	See ! Phantom-like he fades from sight,
	See ! Phantom-like he fades from sight.

The OLD MAN *rises.*

The OLD MAN *goes out.*

INTERLUDE

The MAN OF THE PLACE *approaches the* Shite *Pillar and asks the* PRIEST *to explain the meaning of the strange words he has been saying to himself. At the latter's request the* MAN *tells the story of* SAITŌ-

[1] According to an ancient Chinese belief, the soul is composed of two parts—the heavenly and the earthly—partaking respectively of the *yang* and *yin* principles. After death the soul is resolved into its component parts, the ethereal one returning to heaven, and the sensuous one to earth. See also *Tōboku*, p. 88, note 3.

BETTŌ-SANEMORI'S *last battle and death, whereupon the* PRIEST *informs him that the ghost of the warrior has appeared and conversed with him, and that he proposes to hold prayers for his salvation. After exhorting the people not to fail to attend and requesting a large attendance, the* MAN *goes out.*

PART TWO

1

PRIEST	Let us hold special prayers [1] For the sake of the ghost that haunts this place.	*The* PRIEST *and the* ATTENDANTS *rise.*
PRIEST and ATTENDANTS		
machi-utai	By Shinowara Pond we invoke the Name, By Shinowara Pond we invoke the Name, Utterly trusting in its saving power. Steadily as the moon pursues her westward course, We raise pure voices from first watch until dawn. Our spirits yearn for the Western Paradise, As striking the silver-voiced gongs, Throughout the night	*Go to the centre of the stage.* *The* PRIEST *sits down and joins his hands in prayer.*
PRIEST	We call upon the Name. Namu Amida Butsu ! Namu Amida Butsu !	*Rises and returns to the* Waki *Seat followed by the* ATTENDANTS *who sit down.*

2

While the entrance music deha *is being played, the* GHOST OF SANEMORI *appears and crosses the Bridge-*

---

[1] 'Specified-time prayers,' that is, services performed for some purpose during a fixed period of time, such as one day, seven days or twenty-one days. The practice is still observed.

SANEMORI

way and stands by the Shite *Pillar. He wears a 'smiling old man' mask, tall black cap, long white-hair wig, white head-band, heavy silk kimono, gold-brocade robe, divided skirt and sword.*

SANEMORI   Who can describe how man's heart rejoices,
When he forever leaves this world of woe,
This ancient realm of change,
And gains the land of utmost bliss![1]
Then, so they tell,
His is the land whence there is no return,
His is Buddha's deathless life![2]
A blessed hope springs up in me!
He who without cease repeats the saving prayer

CHORUS   Shall as ceaselessly dwell in Paradise.

SANEMORI   "'Namu,'

CHORUS   I surrender myself to Buddha;

SANEMORI   'Amida,'

CHORUS   Good deeds.
By virtue, therefore, of those words

SANEMORI   Never shall believer fail
To win Amida's Paradise."[3]

CHORUS   O blessed words!

Facing the PRIEST, SANEMORI *joins his hands.*

3

PRIEST   O marvel! See! Across the pond,

[1] Quoted from Eshin Sōzu's treatise entitled *Ōjō Yōshū* (Compendium on Rebirth into Paradise).

[2] From the same. Literally translated, the passage reads: "The place is one from which there is no retrogression. Thus the man who has attained this place has escaped from the three evil worlds and eight obstacles. The life in that land is eternal, so he shall no more taste the pains of birth, age, disease and death."

[3] Quotation from Shan-tao (善導), a famous Chinese priest of the T'ang dynasty. The original, literally translated, reads: "'Namu' means 'surrender myself' and also 'aspiration and dedication'; 'Amida Butsu' means 'necessary deeds.' By virtue of this interpretation of the formula, those who recite it will attain rebirth in Paradise."

Shimmering in the owlet light,
Comes gliding that old man of yesterday,
But see, O wonder! he is clad in armour.

SANEMORI   Like a dead tree sunk in the slime,
Utterly forgotten by the world,
I dwell among the *Asuras*,
Enduring pains too horrible to tell.
O save me from my woe!

PRIEST   You stand before me; I hear your words,
Unheard, unseen of all,

SANEMORI Save by Your Reverence.

PRIEST   The snows of yester-year still linger

SANEMORI Upon the locks and beard of the old warrior,

PRIEST   Attired in splendid robes.

SANEMORI In the unclouded light

PRIEST   Of the setting moon,

SANEMORI In the light of the tapers,

CHORUS   Shimmers his rich brocade,

age-uta   Shimmers his rich brocade.

His armour is joined by green silk braid,
His sword and dagger are enchased with
   gold.
But little does this grandeur profit one,
Who rather craves a Lotus-Seat
In the Lake of Treasure.[1]
In truth, the Way in which we trust,
Like gold untarnished will endure forever.
The oft-repeated golden words[2]
Will surely bear you safe to Paradise,
Will surely bear you safe to Paradise!

---

[1] Descriptions of this lake and other wonders of the Pure Land given in the *Amitabha Sutra* (see p. 42, note 1) and in *Ōjō Yōshū* (see p. 49, note 1) have inspired masterpieces of Buddhist religious art.
[2] I.e. 'Namu Amida Butsu.'

50

4

SANEMORI *kuri*	" Invoke but once Amida's Name, And every sin will melt away." [1]	*Moves to the centre of the stage and sits on a stool.*

CHORUS From earthly things
       Turn aside your mind,
       Aspire to the Buddha-land,
       And free yourself from all attachments !

SANEMORI To-night the time has come
sashi To enter the Way most hard to find.

CHORUS Though I may seem attachment-bound,
       Yet do I make confession as I tell my
         end
       Like to a drop of dew
       Upon the grassy plain of Shinowara.

SANEMORI The battle of Shinowara is lost and Tezuka-
katari no-Tarō-Mitsumori, a Genji warrior, comes
       into the presence of Lord Kiso and says, " I
       have grappled with a strange fellow and cut
       off his head. He cannot have been a general,
       for he had no follower, nor can he be a mere
       soldier for he was wearing a brocade robe.
       Again and again I urged him to declare his
       name but he refused. His speech was that of
       a Kwantō-man." Then Lord Kiso exclaims :
       " Alas ! He must be Saitō-Bettō-Sanemori of
       Nagai. But stay ! His locks and beard should
       be white, and these are raven-black. How
       strange ! Higuchi-no-Jirō knew him well.
       Summon him hither ! " Higuchi comes, takes

---

[1] Words said to occur in Eshin Sōzu's work entitled *Busshin Yōshū* and to be a quotation from the
Ōjō Hōnen Sutra.

one look at the severed head and amid flowing
tears, cries out :

> " O what a cruel sight !
> 'Tis certain this is Saitō-Bettō.
> Sanemori was wont to tell us,
> ' If I, a man of more than sixty years,
> Again should go to war,
> 'Twould ill become my age
> To vie with younger warriors
> And be the first to charge the foe ;
> Yet I would not be an age-worn warrior
> Despised of all.
> So dyeing black my locks and beard,
> In youthful guise I'll fight and die ! '
> In truth he dyed his hair.
> Let some one wash this head and prove
>   it ! "

*Rises from the stool
and goes through the
action of picking up
the head.*

> Scarce has he spoken
> Than taking up the head,

CHORUS   He quits the presence of his lord
> And kneels beside the rippling pond,
> Where mirrored lie
> The weeping willow's green-clad branches.

*SANEMORI goes to
the front of the stage.*

age-uta   " The weather's clearing, and the breeze
> Combs the young tresses of the willow-
>   trees ;
> The water's free from ice, and the waves
> Wash the beard of lake-shore moss." [1]
> And as he laves the locks and beard,
> The dye is washed away,
> And they regain their ancient whiteness.
> The warrior jealous of his renown

*SANEMORI kneels
and goes through the
action of washing the
head.*

[1] Couplet composed by Miyako-no-Yoshika included in the *Wakan-Rōeishū*.

kuse

Should like Sanemori strive to keep it stain-
less.
" O what a noble warrior! "
Exclaim those present, shedding tears.
'Twas not for vanity
I wore this red brocade robe.
Leaving Miyako, I told Lord Munemori;
" The proverb says,
' A man should go back to his birth-place in
brocade.' [1]
I am a native of Echizen,
But during the past years,
While steward of your fief,
I lived at Nagai in Musashi Province.
Now I set out northward
Prepared to die in battle.
If I may wear a robe of scarlet silk,
It will indeed make death beautiful."
On hearing this request my lord
Bestowed on me a robe of red brocade.

SANEMORI Quoting that proverb, the ancient poem
says,
" When, brushing crimson leaves aside,

CHORUS Homeward I wend,
The folk will say,
' Lo, he comes back clad in brocade.' "[2]
In ancient times
'Tis said that Shubaishin [3] of Kwaikei

SANEMORI dances while the following lines are chanted.

[1] Alludes to the ancient Chinese proverb: " If a man becomes a high official and wealthy and yet does not return to his native place, he is like one who goes abroad at night wearing a brocade dress."

[2] Anonymous poem included in the *Gosenshū* (951).

[3] Chinese scholar (Chu Mai-ch'en 朱買臣) who lived in the First Han dynasty. In spite of having to earn a precarious living by hawking fire-wood, he never ceased studying and is credited with reading books even while carrying on his business. His wife who could not bear poverty deserted him. Later

Wore a brocade robe
With flowing sleeves ;
Clad in red brocade
Sanemori left undying memory of his
    valour
Upon the battle-field in North Japan.
Throughout this moonlit night
Till dawn I shall confess my deeds.

5

CHORUS   Yes, make full confession of your deeds,
rongi   Cleansing the waters of your mind
           From all impurities.

SANEMORI Evil attachments long have bound me
           To the *Asura* world,
           And returning here,
           Regret still burns within me
           That, when I tried to grapple Kiso,
           The fellow Tezuka stood between.

Accompanies the chanting of the following lines by rhythmic movements suggesting a battle.

CHORUS   From out their ranks the followers of Kiso
           Come forth and challenge me to battle ;
           Each declaring his name ;
           The first . . .

SANEMORI Tezuka-no-Tarō-Mitsumori.
CHORUS   Seeing his master's danger,
SANEMORI One of his men spurs his horse between us
CHORUS   And dares to grapple with me.
SANEMORI " O lucky fellow, thou hast met
           The bravest warrior in the land ! "
           On to my pommel I bore him down,

he entered government service and was ultimately promoted prefect of Kwaikei (K'uai-chi) Province. The Emperor Wu (140–87 B.C.) who greatly respected him for his wisdom, on one occasion persuaded him to return home attired in his court robes by quoting him the previously-mentioned proverb.

Severed his head, and cast it from me.

CHORUS   Then Tezuka-no-Tarō
Drew near me on the left.
Twice he thrust his sword under the tasset.
We grappled and, together locked,
Crashed to the ground between the
     horses.

SANEMORI   Alas for the old warrior !

CHORUS   Utterly spent with fighting,
Like a dying tree storm-smitten ;
Crushed under Tezuka,
No strength to rise again,
I lay, until his men
Rallying around cut off my head.
Thus at Shinowara I returned to dust,
Leaving no trace behind,
Leaving no trace behind.
Namu Amida Butsu !
O say for me the holy prayers,
O say for me the holy prayers !

SANEMORI *turns towards the* PRIEST, *joins his hands and stamps twice on the stage.*

KIYOTSUNE

CHORUS   Now the foes advance in waves, . . .
—Scene 7.

INTRODUCTION

In some respects *Kiyotsune* departs from the typical *Asura* play which is usually divided into two parts, while this play has only one ; furthermore the *waki* who, as a rule, is a priest on pilgrimage, is here a retainer of the dead hero. Finally, the hero himself does not perform the *kakeri* dance, a very rare case in plays of this group. In addition to such formal deviations from the standard pattern, there are further peculiarities in *Kiyotsune* to which reference will be made later.

The play is built round a very touching incident recorded in the *Heike Monogatari*. After a series of disastrous reverses at the hands of the Genji late in 1183, the Heike army was forced back to the northeastern corner of Kyūshū in the neighbourhood of the famous Hachiman Shrine[1] at Usa. Desiring to know the fate which lay in store for the clan, the leaders requested the god to grant them an oracle. When the god replied that they must give up all hope, Kiyotsune, the third son of Taira-no-Shigemori,[2] who was lieutenant-general of the Left Wing of the Imperial Body-guard, immediately decided to throw himself on the mercy of Buddha and thus ensure his future bliss. Eager to enter the Western Paradise, invoking the name of Amida he leapt one night from his boat into the sea and drowned himself. Subsequently a lock of his hair was discovered in the boat apparently cut off by him and left as a keepsake for his wife in Miyako, which his faithful retainer, Awazu-no-Saburō, took upon himself to deliver.

The feelings of mingled sorrow and resentment aroused in Kiyotsune's wife by the news of her husband's suicide, lead up to a moving scene between her and the ghost of Kiyotsune which appears to her in a dream. The play ends with a remarkable dance performed by Kiyotsune's ghost in which he evokes the strife-torn world of the *Asuras* described by the chorus. In answer to his tenfold

---

[1] Ancient Shinto shrine in Buzen Province, Kyūshū, dedicated to the Emperor Ōjin. In the ninth century, in accordance with an oracle, another shrine was built near Kyoto known as Otoko-yama Hachiman, which came to be especially revered by the Genji as the shrine of their patron deity just as that on Miyajima in the Inland Sea was by the Heike clan.

[2] Unlike his father Kiyomori who was a typical dictator, Shigemori was righteous, merciful and refined, and tried to restrain his father's policy of violence. After his son's death at a comparatively early age, Kiyomori gave full rein to his inordinate lust for power which ultimately led to the downfall of the family.

invocation of Amida[1] at the time of his death Kiyotsune, purified at last from all thoughts of hate, enters the Western Paradise by virtue of the saving vow of Amida.

The main theme of the present drama might perhaps best be described as the strife of love and death in a dream. These two motives not only dominate, but provide the main dramatic interest, which is further enhanced by the tragic historical events which destroyed the wedded happiness of Kiyotsune's wife who was separated from her husband, first by the war and then by his wilful and seemingly unnecessary suicide. The play also develops not less clearly but with greater subtlety than other Noh plays the underlying Buddhistic theme that it is only through faith in the Great Vow of Amida that man can escape rebirth and achieve ultimate blessedness.

As regards its production, the following points are worth noting because of their dramatic significance. At the beginning of the dream the *waki* (Awazu-no-Saburō), instead of leaving the stage by the Bridgeway, as is customary, retires through the Sliding Door. When the *shite* (Kiyotsune) appears in his wife's dream towards the end of the scene, he enters softly while the chorus is singing, thus indicating the passage from reality to dream. The *tsure* (Kiyotsune's wife) remains on the stage throughout the performance, while the *waki*, contrary to the general practice in most Noh plays, only appears in the earlier part. In the later scenes only two persons are on the stage, the *tsure* (who never moves from the *Waki* Seat) and the *shite*. Since the latter is really a dream figure existing only in the wife's imagination and not a real ghost, the whole play may be regarded, in effect, as a one-person play. Finally, the absence of the *kyōgen* is due to the fact that, apart from its being a one-act play, a comic interlude would introduce a discordant note and destroy the emotional tension created by the dream-scene.

Author : Zeami Motokiyo (1363–1443)
Source : *Gempei Seisuiki* (History of the Rise and Fall of the Genji and the Heike), Vol. XXXIII: ' Episode of Kiyotsune's Suicide '; *Heike Monogatari* (Tale of the Heike), Vol. VIII: ' The Heike's Evacuation from the Dazaifu.'

---

[1] According to the tenets of the Amidist sects prevalent in those days, tenfold repetition just before death of the formula ' Namu Amida Butsu ' (I put all my faith in Amida Buddha) had the power to ensure the immediate rebirth into the Western Paradise.

KIYOTSUNE

Persons

WIFE OF KIYOTSUNE   *Tsure*
AWAZU-NO-SABURŌ   *Waki*
GHOST OF KIYOTSUNE   *Shite*

Place

Hiding-place of Kiyotsune's wife in Miyako

Season

Late autumn

WIFE OF KIYOTSUNE *appears on the Bridgeway and advancing across it, enters the stage and sits on the* Waki *Seat. She wears a* tsure *mask, wig, painted gold-patterned under-kimono and brocade outer-kimono.*

1

While the entrance music shidai *is being played,* AWAZU-NO-SABURŌ *appears, crosses the Bridgeway and stops by the* Shite *Pillar. He wears a striped kimono,* kake-suō *robe, white broad divided skirt, short sword, mushroom hat and amulet-bag hanging from his neck.*

AWAZU	Crossing the surges of the eightfold sea,
shidai	Crossing the surges of the eightfold sea,
	I must return to where the Court

Stands within its nine gates.[1]

CHORUS
jidori
Crossing the surges of the eightfold sea,
I must return to where the Court
Stands within its nine gates.

AWAZU

I am a retainer of the late Kiyotsune, Lieutenant-General of the Left Wing of the Imperial Body-guard. Awazu-no-Saburō is my name. My late master was defeated in the battles in Tsukushi,[2] and since his retreat to Miyako was cut off, he probably preferred to take his own life rather than perish at the hands of the common soldiery no better than wayside weeds. So, late one moonlit night, he plunged from his boat into the sea off the coast of Yanagi.[3] Later, when searching the boat, I found a lock of hair he had left behind him as a keepsake. Having undeservedly escaped with my life, I am now carrying this keepsake to his wife in Miyako.

michi-yuki

In recent years
I have lived a country life,
I have lived a country life.
My heart is filled with sadness,
Since, when I return,
Miyako's glorious springtide no more will greet me.
Past is mournful autumn,
And the wintry rain
Beats down upon my dress.
Grieving at my unhappy fate,

---

[1] See *Tamura*, p. 24, note 1.
[2] Ancient name for Kyūshū now rarely used.
[3] Town on the eastern coast of Buzen Province.

My sleeves are drenched with tears,
As in disguise my journey I pursue,
As in disguise my journey I pursue.
Travelling in haste, I have quickly reached Miyako.

Retiring to the Stage-attendants' Seat, removes his mushroom hat and slipping the amulet-bag inside the fold of his kimono, moves to the Shite *Pillar.*

2

AWAZU   A visitor is announcing his arrival. It is Awazu-no-Saburō just come from Tsukushi. Please announce him.

Turns towards the Waki *Seat.*

WIFE   What? Is it you, Awazu-no-Saburō? You need not be announced. Pray enter. What message do you bring me from my lord?

AWAZU   A message I am loath to deliver to my lady.

WIFE   A message you are loath to deliver? Has my lord perchance renounced the world?

Kneeling in the centre of the stage, and placing both hands on the floor, makes a deep obeisance.

AWAZU   No, he has not renounced the world.

WIFE   I have heard he has come safely through the recent battles in Tsukushi.

AWAZU   Yes, my lady, he has come safely through the recent battles in Tsukushi. But since his way to Miyako was cut off, my lord thought to put an end to his own life rather than lose it at the hands of nameless soldiery no better than wayside weeds and while we were off the coast of Yanagi in Buzen Province, late one moonlit night, he leapt overboard and was drowned.

WIFE   What! You mean he cast himself into the sea?
Never can I forgive him such an end!
Had he in battle perished

Or died of illness,
I could resign myself to fate ;
But that he himself should seek
A watery grave
Proves all his vows
Were lying words.
Oh ! Woe is me,
Naught's left me in this world
Save my vain rancour against my lord !

CHORUS   How dream-like now appear
sage-uta   Our wedded joys !
age-uta   Through all these troubled years[1]
             I've hid from prying eyes,
             I've hid from prying eyes—
             My sobs voiceless as the rustle of *susuki*
                grass[2]
             Swayed by autumn winds
             In the hedge round my dwelling.
             From whom need I to-day conceal my
                grief?
             Like to the cuckoo[3]
             Crying until the moon-beams
             Grow pale in the dawn sky,
             Freely and openly I'll weep,
             Freely and openly I'll weep !

---

[1] Allusion to the period following the abandonment of Miyako by the Heike in the autumn of 1183 and its occupation by the Genji troops. At that time Kiyotsune's wife was forced by her parents to remain in Miyako instead of following her lord into the west. The death of Kiyotsune took place three years later.

[2] *Miscanthus sinensis* : wild grass somewhat resembling pampas grass and found all over Japan. It reaches five or six feet in height, and in autumn puts forth tassel-like flowers.

[3] I.e. *hototogisu*, the Japanese species of the cuckoo genus which comes to Japan from the south in late spring and leaves in autumn. Unlike its Western relative, its cry consists of several notes instead of two and is often heard at night.

AWAZU   Later I searched the boat and found this
lock of my lord's hair left you as a keepsake.
Pray gaze on it and soothe your grieving
heart.

*Places the amulet-
bag on his fan and offers
it to KIYOTSUNE's
wife, who takes it.*

WIFE   Is this the raven lock of my
        late lord?
      My eyes are blinded,
      My spirit longs for its release
      And ever stronger grows my yearning.
      " Each time I look upon this lock
      Grief tears at my heart ;
      I bid it hence return
      Unto my sorrow's fountain-head."[1]

CHORUS   As she repeats these lines,
sage-uta   The keepsake she returns
      And seeks her couch.
      All through the night
      Tears of longing fall,
      The while she prays that he may come to
        her
      If but in dream.
      Sleepless, in vain her pillow oft she shifts ;
      Yet ever stronger grows her longing,
      Yet ever stronger grows her longing.

*KIYOTSUNE's wife
places the amulet-bag
on the floor.*

*Soon after the CHO-
RUS begins, AWAZU
retires through the Slid-
ing Door.*

3

The GHOST OF KIYOTSUNE, *who has appeared
during the last chorus, advances and stands by the*

---

[1] The original contains a number of pivot-words which baffle any attempt at literal translation,
such as " tsukushi " (to grieve or place-name), " kami " (hair or god) and " usa " (grief or the Shinto
shrine of that name. Cf. p. 59).

First Pine. He wears a chūjō *mask, long black-hair wig, white head-band, tall black cap, embroidered kimono, gold-brocade robe with left shoulder uncovered, white broad divided skirt and sword.*

KIYOTSUNE
sashi

'Tis said : " The sage is dream-free,"[1]
Yet for whom is life reality?
" A mote within the eye
May cause a man to feel
The threefold world too small ;
But when his mind is free from care,
His couch seems vaster than the world."[2]
Past griefs are truly but illusion
And present sadness but a dream ;
Which, like drifting cloud or running water,
Do pass away, leaving no trace.
O poor frail self that clings unto this world !
" Since once I saw my lover in a dream,
I've learned to trust in dreams."[3]
O thou whom I once loved !
Kiyotsune is here !

Advancing on to the stage, stands before his WIFE.

WIFE

O wondrous marvel !
I see Kiyotsune by my pillow,
And yet I know that he has drowned himself.
How then can I behold him save
 in dream?
Though but a dream,
Yet I am thankful
To see his form once more.

---

[1] Quotation from Ta-hui Sung-kao (大慧宋杲) (1089–1163), a Chinese monk of the Zen sect. The same saying in a slightly altered form is traceable to Chuang-tse (莊子).
[2] Quoted from a Chinese poem by Musō Kokushi (1275–1351), a Japanese monk of the Zen sect.
[3] Poem by Ono-no-Komachi included in the *Kokinshū*.

But since, defying heaven's decree,
You brought your life to an untimely end,
You've proved yourself untrue
And bred resentment in my breast.

KIYOTSUNE   Though you reproach me for my deed,
You too are not unworthy of reproach.
Why did you spurn the keepsake I left to
ease your pain?

WIFE   No! No! Why I did so
Is set forth in a poem
Which scarce conveys
How deep the sight of it did stir me.
" Each time I look upon this lock,
Grief tears at my heart;
I bid it hence return

KIYOTSUNE Unto my sorrow's fountain-head."
Unless you had grown weary of my love,
you should have treasured the gift I took such
care to leave you.

WIFE   You mistake my reason:
You meant the keepsake as a comfort,
But as I look upon that lock
My mind becomes unruly like my hair.

KIYOTSUNE Since you have spurned my gift and rendered vain my thoughtful care, I cannot forgive your cruelty.

WIFE   Nor I your wilful death.
KIYOTSUNE   One taunts the other with reproaches,
WIFE   The other tauntingly replies.
KIYOTSUNE   The keepsake is a source of woe.
WIFE   And a lock of hair
CHORUS   Becomes for us a source of strife,
age-uta   Becomes for us a source of strife.

67

To-night the two lie side by side,
Each head pillowed on the other's arm,
Wet by tears of anger ;
Estranged by anger, though in body joined,
Sadly they lie as if they slept alone.
" The keepsake brings new agony,
Recalls afresh to the bereaved
The loss she had else forgot," [1]
And makes salt tears to flow,
And makes salt tears to flow.

Both weep.

4

KIYOTSUNE Listen while I tell you what befell me in   *Advances to the cen-*
            the days gone by, and forget your grievance.   *tre, and sits down on*
                                                           a stool.
sashi   Hearken to me !
            We chanced to learn
            The foe was marching through Kyūshū
            Against our castle in Yamaga.[2]
            Dismayed, in haste we took to barges,
            Plying our oars the long night through,
            And reached Yanagi in Buzen Province.
CHORUS   Where, as its name bespeaks,
            An avenue of willows lines the sea-front ;
            Here rude buildings were put up
            To house the Imperial Court.
KIYOTSUNE   Then we were told
            The Emperor would invoke Hachiman
            At Usa Shrine ;
CHORUS   Thither a store of gold and silver
            And countless precious gifts,

---

[1] Anonymous poem included in the *Kokinshū.*

[2] Situated in Chikuzen Province. The Heike when forced to abandon their base at the Dazaifu were given an asylum by the local lord in this castle.

	And seven steeds sacred to the god,
	Were brought as offerings to the Lord of War.[1]
WIFE	Though you may think I still reproach you,
	Was it not a rash and foolish deed
	To cast away your life before the time,
	While yet you knew not
	The fate awaiting the Emperor and the Heike clan?
KIYOTSUNE	Truly you would be right,
	Had not the sacred oracle declared
	Our cause past hope.
	But pray, hear me to the end!
CHORUS	How while the Emperor and his court
	Were keeping vigil at the shrine,
	Offering up prayers and making vows,
	Behind the curtain of brocade
	That hangs before the holy place,
	A voice divine proclaimed,—
KIYOTSUNE	" No power hath the God of Usa
	To change man's hateful fate on earth!
	What serves it then to urge Him further? "
CHORUS	" Now the last hope
	Grows faint as insects' dying song;
	Forlorn indeed is autumn's eve! "[2]

5

KIYOTSUNE	Alas! Gods and Buddhas
CHORUS	Both forsake our cause.
	All confidence and spirit lost,
	Like a rumbling cart

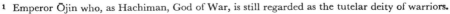

[1] Emperor Ōjin who, as Hachiman, God of War, is still regarded as the tutelar deity of warriors.
[2] Poem by Fujiwara-no-Shunzei included in the *Senzaishū*

The Emperor we follow to his quarters.
O woeful sight !

kuse   Meanwhile we learn
The foe is marching into Nagato Province.
Once more we embark,
Wretched indeed our plight !

KIYOTSUNE *leaves the stool and dances while the following lines are chanted.*

Life is an ever-changing dream,
And those who once in the Hōgen era[1]
Rioted like flowers in spring,
Now, in the Juei autumn,[2]
Alas, are scattered
Like sere and yellow leaves
Over the waves,
Each leaf, a boat.
Snowy-crested billows
Urged by the autumn wind from Yanagi
Are like a pursuing host.
A glimpse of herons caught

Amidst the distant pines
Makes their spirit quail,
Thinking they might be
The snow-white pennants of the Genji host.
Now as I ponder deeply
Wherefore Hachiman's fateful words
Run ever in my head,
I, Kiyotsune, call to mind
That in the head of an upright man
God dwells.[3]

---

[1] During this era (1156–1158) the Heike took over the political ascendancy previously enjoyed by the Fujiwara nobles.

[2] Autumn of 1183. See p. 64, note 1. The Heike took with them the young Emperor, nephew of Munemori, head of the clan.

[3] Supposed to have been the vow made by Hachiman, meaning that he would always guide and protect a just man.

KIYOTSUNE

Possessed by that single thought,
I feel 'twould be but foolishness
To save the dew-drop of my foredoomed
    life,

CHORUS

As though it could endure.
Rather than trust to any boat
Floating like seaweed to and fro,
A prey to endless sorrow,
Like to a water-fowl
I'll dive into the sea,
And so end my life.

Keeping my own counsel
I stand and wait
Upon the bow-planks
While the autumn moon
Grows pale in the dawning sky.
Drawing forth my flute,
I blow a few clear silvery notes,
Then sing *imayō*[1] songs

And chant some ancient verses.
Musing upon the past and future,
Well do I see that soon or late,
The glorious past forgot,
The present full of woe,
Perish I must

Like surf upon the shore.
Our life is but a travail
And I can quit this world without regret.
Others may deem my deed stark mad;
Well, let them judge me as they will!

---

[1] Song consisting of eight alternating lines of seven and five syllables, first invented and very popular throughout the Heian period (794-1184).

The moon descends the western sky,
I'll follow her to the Western Paradise.
Namu Amida Butsu! Receive my spirit!
Thus praying, overboard I leap
And sink down to the oozy bottom of the
    sea.
So pitifully ends my woeful life!

*KIYOTSUNE sinks
weeping by the Shite
Pillar.*

6

WIFE   Hearing your tale, my mind is mazed;
             Sobs shake me
             And hot tears fall.
             O tragic ending to our wedded life!   *Weeps.*

KIYOTSUNE How true the saying,
             " Once fallen in the pit
             The selfsame grievous lot
             Awaits all men." [1]

7

KIYOTSUNE Where'er I turn   *Rises and dances*
             In the *Asura* world,   *while the following
                                   lines are chanted.*

CHORUS   Where'er I turn
             In the *Asura* world,
             The trees are foes,
             Arrows the falling rain,
             Sharp swords strew the ground,
             The hills are iron castles,
             The clouds are battle-pennants,   *KIYOTSUNE draws*
             Enemies thrust with their proud blades, *his sword.*

---

[1] It is said that when Nichizō Shōnin (886–985), a monk of the Hossō sect, visited Hell guided by Bodhisattva Zao, he saw the Emperor Daigo, famed for his benevolence, being tormented in the lake of molten iron. In answer to the monk's surprised enquiry why he was there, the Emperor repeated the lines quoted.

Hate flashing in their eyes.
Here all is strife:
Anger and lust,
Greed and ignorance
Strive against the Holy Way;
Blind attachment and Buddha-nature
Grapple together.[1]
Now the foes advance in waves,
Now like the ebbing tide retreat.
The battles of Shikoku and Kyūshū
Endlessly are fought again
Till, now at last, these torments cease.
Relying utterly upon the Barque of Holy
    Law,
The dying Kiyotsune uttered the tenfold
    prayer:
Kiyotsune, the 'Pure'-hearted,
Kiyotsune, the 'Pure'-hearted
Now enters the Western Paradise.
Praised be Amida!

KIYOTSUNE *throws down his sword.*

KIYOTSUNE *stamps twice on the stage at the* Shite Seat.

[1] These five lines are a tentative translation. The original passage is so corrupt that no satisfactory interpretation has yet been reached.

73

TŌBOKU

CHORUS   "I am
The mistress of the plum-tree."
              —Part I, scene 4.

INTRODUCTION

Tōboku is a *kazura-mono*. The plays of this group contain a *jo-no-mai* dance performed to the accompaniment of hand-drums and, in some cases, a horizontal drum. In *Tōboku*, however, only hand-drums are used, the reason for this being that these hand-drums best stimulate the *yūgen*[1] mood characteristic of *kazura-mono*.

The present play is designed to illustrate the romantic temperament of Lady Izumi,[2] a poetess endowed with rare poetic sensibility. While attached to the Lady of Shōtō-mon-in she gained considerable notoriety because of her love-affairs with several princes. The Lady of Shōtō-mon-in was by name Shōshi, daughter of Fujiwara-no-Michinaga known as the Midō-no-Kwampaku[3] who exercised a dominating influence at the Heian court. Upon becoming the Emperor Ichijō's consort, Shōshi went to live in a pavilion known as the Tōboku-in on the northeastern side of the precincts of the Hōjō-ji Temple situated in the northeastern quarter of Miyako where Michinaga lived. The suite of rooms occupied by Lady Izumi was at the west end of the Tōboku-in outside which she was said to have planted a plum-tree.

When the play opens many years have passed since the death of Lady Izumi and the former palace has become a temple, but her plum-tree (' Plum-tree-by-the-Eaves ') still puts forth its lovely blossoms as of old.

After death, having through her poetry attained enlightenment, she became one of the Bodhisattvas of Song and Dance in the Western Paradise. Such is the legend around which the author has built the present play. Drawn by the

[1] See General Introduction, p. xii.

[2] Celebrated beauty, a daughter of Ōe-no-Masamune. She first married Tachibana-no-Michisada, prefect of Izumi Province, and by him had a daughter, named Lady Koshikibu, who was also a famous poetess. Having divorced shortly afterwards, Izumi fell in love with the third son of the Emperor Reizei and after his death three years later, she became attached to his younger brother Prince Atsumichi. The course of this love-affair is related in *Lady Izumi's Diary*. After the death of her young lover, she entered the service of the Lady of Shōtō-mon-in and subsequently married Fujiwara-no-Masayasu whom she accompanied to his post in Tango Province, but later divorced. At the close of her life she became a nun in Miyako where she died.

[3] Literally ' emperor's chief counsellor of the temple,' so called because he built the magnificent Buddhist temple of Hōjō-ji. He served four successive emperors in the capacity of regent, chief counsellor and prime minister between 996 and 1015.

77

memory of those bygone days, Izumi's ghost appears in a vision to the travelling monk who is visiting the ancient garden of the Tōboku-in to admire and praise the 'Plum-tree-by-the Eaves,' and tells him that she has attained Buddhahood by virtue of the *Lotus Sutra*. *Yūgen* pervades the latter part of the play, reaching its highest expression in the *jo-no-mai* dance performed by the ghost of Lady Izumi.

    Author: Zeami Motokiyo (1363–1443)
    Source: Unknown.

TŌBOKU

Persons

Monk from the Eastland	*Waki*
Two Attendants	*Waki-zure*
Man of the Place	*Kyōgen*
Maiden	*Shite* in Part One
Ghost of Lady Izumi	*Shite* in Part Two

Place

Tōboku-in in Miyako

Season

New Year

PART ONE

1

While the entrance music shidai *is being played, the* Monk from the Eastland *with* Two Attendants *appears and enters the stage. He wears a pointed hood, plain kimono and broad-sleeved robe. The* Two Attendants *are also similarly attired.*

Monk and Attendants

shidai	The New Year ushers in the spring,
	The New Year ushers in the spring.
	Let us hasten towards flowery Miyako.
Chorus	The New Year ushers in the spring,
jidori	Let us hasten towards flowery Miyako.

MONK   I am an Eastland monk. As I have not yet seen Miyako, I have decided to journey thither this spring.

MONK and ATTENDANTS

michi-yuki   This morning we crossed the Barrier of Mists,[1]

This morning we crossed the Barrier of Mists,

While the spring haze was rising,

Wending our way across Musashi Plain;[2]

Leaving it far behind us,

Crossing mountain upon cloud-encircled mountain,

Hither have we come;

As we near Miyako,

The travellers' hearts rejoice,

The travellers' hearts rejoice.

MONK   Travelling in haste, we have reached Miyako earlier than we expected. Look at that plum-tree in full bloom. Surely it must be a famous tree. I will ask its name from someone in the neighbourhood.

ATTENDANTS Pray do so.

They proceed to the Waki Seat and sit down.

2

MONK   Is anyone about?

Turns towards the Bridgeway.

The MAN OF THE PLACE *who has been sitting on the* Kyōgen *Seat rises and approaches the First Pine. He wears a striped kimono, sleeveless robe and trailing divided skirt, and short sword.*

---

[1] I.e. Kasumi-ga-seki situated at Tama Village, Musashi Province. The village is on the banks of the river Tama, west of Tokyo.

[2] Southern part of the Kantō plain, one of the widest plains in Japan.

MAN OF THE PLACE

Were you calling me? What do you want?

MONK   We have come to see the sights of Miyako for the first time. I see an exceedingly beautiful plum-tree in the garden. Please tell me if it is famous.

MAN OF THE PLACE

Certainly it is. It was planted long ago by Lady Izumi and is called 'Izumi Shikibu' after her. Please look at it as long as you like.

MONK   Thank you kindly for telling me. I will sit yonder and quietly enjoy its beauty.

MAN OF THE PLACE

If you need me, please call.

MONK   I am much obliged.

MAN OF THE PLACE

At your service.

Returns to the Kyōgen Seat while the MONK advances to the centre of the stage and faces the Front audience and then starts walking towards the Waki Seat.

MONK   So this is the plum-tree 'Izumi Shikibu.' I shall sit awhile and gaze at it.

3

The MAIDEN *comes out of the Mirror Room, wearing a 'young woman' mask, wig, painted gold-patterned under-kimono and brocade outer-kimono.*

MAIDEN   Excuse me, reverend monk. What were you told when you enquired about the plum-tree?

MONK   Well, when I enquired, I was told that it bears the name 'Izumi Shikubu.'

MAIDEN   No. You should rather call it by such names as Kōbun-boku[1] or Ōshuku-bai.[2] You must not

Stands on the Waki Seat and faces the MAIDEN.

---

[1] 'Love-of-learning tree,' poetic name given to the plum-tree, derived from an anecdote which tells how plum-trees produced unusually beautiful blossoms during the reign of an ancient emperor of China when pursuit of learning flourished and how it ceased to do so when learning was neglected.

[2] 'Spring-warbler-nestling plum,' name given to a particular tree belonging to a daughter of the famous

believe what an ignorant person tells you. It
is said that when this temple was still the
palace of the Shōtō-mon-in, Lady Izumi
planted this tree and called it 'Plum-tree-by-
the-Eaves' and never tired of gazing upon its
blossoms.

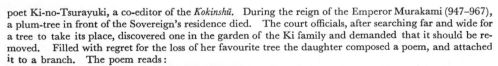

> Since you have the good fortune
> Of seeing the marvellous blossoms,
> Would you recite the *Lotus Sutra?*
> Though you are not related to her,
> It will help her soul.

This is the 'Plum-tree-by-the-Eaves' planted
by Lady Izumi.

MONK   So this is the 'Plum-tree-by-the Eaves'
planted by Lady Izumi! Then here is where
Lady Izumi used to live?

MAIDEN   Yes, it is. Lady Izumi's rooms have been *Enters the stage*
preserved untouched to this day and always *and stands by the*
attract many visitors. *Shite Pillar.*

MONK   How wonderful this plum-tree
That tells of her who planted it,

MAIDEN   Whose scent and hue,
For love of its one-time mistress,
Yearly grow richer.

MONK   Its beauty and grace

MAIDEN   Still

MONK   Recall her long since dead.

poet Ki-no-Tsurayuki, a co-editor of the *Kokinshū*. During the reign of the Emperor Murakami (947–967),
a plum-tree in front of the Sovereign's residence died. The court officials, after searching far and wide for
a tree to take its place, discovered one in the garden of the Ki family and demanded that it should be removed. Filled with regret for the loss of her favourite tree the daughter composed a poem, and attached
it to a branch. The poem reads:

> I submit to the august order
> With deepest reverence,
> But what shall I tell the warbler,
> When it asks about its accustomed nest?

CHORUS
age-uta

Defying passing years,
This ancient ' Plum-tree-by-the-Eaves,'
This ancient ' Plum-tree-by-the-Eaves '
Is faithful to its mistress.
As whirling snow-flakes fill the sky,
So does her fame,
Borne on the wings of her flower-like fancies,
Reach unto every corner of this land.

4

CHORUS
rongi

Listening to this ancient tale,
I well believe all round me here
Unchanged remains,
As in the spring days now long past.
I alone feel like a stranger here [1]—

MAIDEN

Not you alone perhaps.
Of whom, indeed, should you enquire
Concerning past things
Save only me?
Though I am no longer of this world,
Fleeting as a dew-drop on the wayside grass,
I still dwell within this flowering tree.

CHORUS

You say, you dwell among these flowers.
But blossoms fall from branches,
Like birds seeking again their
ancient nests,

MAIDEN

Returning whence they once did
come.

CHORUS

Then your life's journey's ended?

[1] Allusion to a poem by Ariwara-no-Narihira in the *Kokinshū*, which reads:
> Is the moon changed?
> Is spring no longer
> What it was of yore,
> While I remain my old self?

MAIDEN	Under the shadow of the flowers
CHORUS	" I seem to rest. I am
	The mistress of the plum-tree."
	Then in the sunset glow
	She melts into the shadow of the tree,
	She melts into the shadow of the tree.

The MAIDEN *goes out.*

INTERLUDE

The MAN OF THE PLACE *enters. In reply to the* MONK'S *request, he tells him the story of the* Tōboku-in, *of the ' Plum-tree-by-the-Eaves,' and the Hōjō Hall.*[1]

PART TWO

1

MONK and ATTENDANTS
machi-utai   All through the night
Under the ' Plum-tree-by-the-Eaves,'
Under the ' Plum-tree-by-the-Eaves,'
Its blossoms like the Wondrous Law[2]
While the moon steers
Her unerring westward course,
We chant the Holy Sutra,
We chant the Holy Sutra.

---

[1] ' Ten-feet-square,' a chief priest's living quarters in a Buddhist temple, named after the room of a famous lay Buddhist Wei-mo (維摩), the central figure of the *Wei-mo Sutra*. The scripture tells how when Wei-mo was ill, Buddha sent his greatest disciples to enquire after his health. Before their arrival Wei-mo, by means of his miraculous powers, enlarged his cottage to accommodate thirty-two thousand seats. Subsequently, to the wonderment of his visitors, he expounded to them the most recondite doctrines of Mahayana Buddhism.

[2] Allusion to the title of the *Lotus Sutra*, which is in full the Sutra of the Lotus of the Wondrous Law, the name consisting, as in many other cases, of the plain mention of the subject-matter and the metaphorical description of the thing.

84

2

While the entrance music issei *is being played, the*
GHOST OF LADY Izumi *enters the stage and stands
by the* Shite *Pillar. She wears a 'young woman'
mask, wig, painted gold-patterned under-kimono, dancing* chōken *robe and scarlet broad divided skirt.*

LADY   Blessed be the Sutra,
Blessed be the Sutra !
Your reading of the Book of Parables[1] brings
back to my mind an incident which took place
while I was still in this world. When this was
still the Shōtō-mon-in, the Midō-no-Kwampaku
rode by the gate in his carriage,[2] reciting
aloud the Parables of the *Lotus Sutra.* Inside the
gate, I, Shikibu, hearing it, composed this
poem:
    " When without the gate
    I hear the ' Wheels of the Law ' rolling by,
    From the ' Burning House '[3]
    I too am set free."
Now your chanting of the Sutra
Brings that day back to me.

MONK   In truth 'tis Lady Izumi's poem,
Known and repeated through the land.
Were you, as the poem says,
Truly set free from the ' Burning House ? '

LADY   In very truth, I was. Fled from the ' Burn-

---

[1] I.e. third chapter of the *Lotus Sutra.*

[2] Ox-carriage. Even at the present time it is customary for the hearse at the Imperial funeral to be drawn by oxen.

[3] The threefold world of desire, form and non-form in which the soul of man is destined to trans-migrate until it is saved, is compared to a house on fire. This well-known parable is told in the third chapter of the *Lotus Sutra.*

ing House,' but by virtue of my poetry I have
now become a Bodhisattva of Song and Dance,

MONK	And still live in this temple,
LADY	Though saved from the ' Burning House.'
MONK	And
LADY	Now
CHORUS	Leaving the threefold world of suffering,
age-uta	Crossing the threshold of the ' Burning House,'
	Borne by the ' Three Vehicles of the Law,'¹
	Lady Izumi has attained to Buddhahood.
	Let us give thanks !

3

CHORUS	Poetry is indeed a sermon
kuri	Preached by the ' Body-of-Law.'²
	The memory of poets alone lives on for ever,³
	So writes Ki-no-Tsurayuki.
LADY	Poetry moves the Heavens and Earth,
sashi	And melts the Demon's heart.⁴
CHORUS	To her incline their ear both Gods and Buddhas ;

¹ In the above-mentioned parable the three vehicles are described as being drawn respectively by sheep, deer and oxen, symbolizing the three ways of salvation preached in Hinayana (lesser vehicle) Buddhism. According to the *Lotus Sutra*, however, Buddha really bestows on his believers a single coach drawn by huge milk-white bulls, symbolizing Mahayana (greater vehicle) Buddhism.

² The all-comprehensive absolute principle of the universe — corresponding in some respects to God-the-Father—which together with the Body-of-Reward acquired by a buddha upon attaining supreme enlightenment through the practice of all disciplines and good deeds in the course of innumerable lives, and the Body-of-Transformation assumed by a buddha to save the world forms the Buddhist Trinity.

³ Quotation from the Chinese preface to the *Kokinshū*, written by Ki-no-Yoshimochi : " The vulgar vie with one another in seeking after fame and wealth and are indifferent to poetry. Alas ! even if they rise to become ministers or generals or accumulate vast riches, they ultimately die and are forgotten even before their remains have decomposed in the grave. . . . "

⁴ Another quotation from the preface : " There is nothing like poetry for moving heaven and earth, appealing to gods and demons, edifying people, harmonizing man and wife."

The verse inspired by Miyako
Flower-decked beneath a tender sky,
Springing from a poet's heart,
Fulfils the ' Way of Heaven.'

kuse

LADY IZUMI *dances while the following lines are chanted.*

This holy temple guards from demon-hosts
The perilous northeast quarter[1] of Mi-
yako ;
The soothing voices of Kamo's flowing
waters[2]
Rising among the wooded northern hills,
And of Shirakawa's ending none knows
where,
Sow in the mind
The seed of rebirth in the Land of Bliss.
Within the garden lies a brimming pond.
" Birds nest in the islet's trees,
A monk knocks at the moonlit gate,"[3]
Through which a ceaseless stream of people
flows
Apparelled in bright hues—
A sight that can alone be seen
In glorious Miyako in bloom-time.

LADY — Worshippers of Buddha
Who hearken to his words,

CHORUS — Come and go, morn and night,
In ever-growing multitudes.

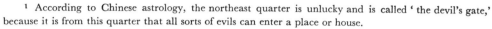

[1] According to Chinese astrology, the northeast quarter is unlucky and is called ' the devil's gate,' because it is from this quarter that all sorts of evils can enter a place or house.

[2] River which, springing from the mountains northwest of Kyoto, and flowing through the eastern part of the city, with several other large streams forms the Yodo which empties itself into the Bay of Osaka.

[3] Quotation rom a poem by the Chinese poet Chia Tao (賈島; 788–843) famous for the infinite pains he took in polishing his verse. It is said that the word *knock* in the lines quoted was only decided upon after pondering long whether the word *push* should not be used in preference to *knock*.

The pine-trees
In the valley's depths
Soughing in the early autumn breeze,
Tell us summer's ninety-days are o'er
And that all-withering autumn is here,
Awakening man to the 'Way of
  Truth.'[1]

The moon, mirrored in the waters of the
  pond,
Images the Buddha
Who, to save mankind,
Came down to earth.[2]

In this fair garden of Tōboku-in
Four seasons ruled by *yang* and *yin*[3]
Are seen in their full beauty.

4

CHORUS   In the spring night,

LADY IZUMI *performs a* jo-no-mai *dance.*

LADY   In the spring night   *Continues to dance*
         Darkness cannot prevail,   *while the following*
                                       lines are chanted.
         For the plum blossom,
CHORUS   Unseen though be its hue,
         Fills the night with fragrance,
         Fills the night with fragrance,
         Fills the night with fragrance.[4]

[1,2] Two expressions usually combined and forming a single Buddhist maxim: " To seek after the highest knowledge and to devote oneself to the salvation of others."

[3] In Chinese philosophy the whole universe is reduced to two fundamental elements or principles, the positive *yang* and the negative *yin*. The nature of everything is determined by the predominance of one or other of these elements in its composition, its behaviour depending upon the combined influence of the same principles. As applied to the seasons, spring and summer are dominated by *yang*, while autumn and winter are ruled by *yin*.

[4] Quotation from a poem by Ōshikōchi-no-Mitsune in the *Kokinshū*.

5

LADY   Though to recall those days of yore
                When, urged by hues and scents,
                I was passion's slave,
CHORUS   Is now unseemly,
                Yet memory still makes me repine
                    them—
                I must depart
                Lest strangers see my worthless tears.

LADY   Fare you well !
                The flower returns whence it sprang,
CHORUS   Fare you well !
                The flower returns whence it sprang,
                The bird returns to its old nest,[1]
                I too return to my old home.
                Though men might think
                The lamp-lit Hōjō Hall
                To be the ' Burning House,'
                In truth it is the Lotus-Seat,

                Where now Lady Izumi dwells—
                And as she glides
                Within her chamber in the Hōjō Hall,
                The monk awakens from his dream,
                The monk awakens from his dream.

LADY IZUMI *stamps twice on the stage at the* Shite *Seat.*

---

[1] Allusion to the Emperor Sutoku's poem in the *Senzaishū*, which reads :
        The blossoms return to the foot of the tree,
        And the birds to their nest,
        But none knows
        Where spring goes.

89

IZUTSU

(WELL-CURB)

CHORUS It does not look like a woman,
        But a man—the living image of Narihira.
                        —Part II, scene 3.

INTRODUCTION

Izutsu is a *kazura-mono* or 'female-wig' play in which the *jo-no-mai* dance is accompanied by a large and a small hand-drum.

About a thousand years ago there lived two famous lovers: Ariwara-no-Narihira, one of the Six Major Poets[1] of the Early Heian Period (794–930), and the daughter of Ki-no-Aritsune. Narihira who came of a princely family and was known not less for his gallantry than for his poetry, has since become a legendary figure. In this play, however, the Narihira legend is greatly modified. As children, hero and heroine were neighbours. Outside the gate of one of their houses was a well, and the children used to lean over its wooden curb (*izutsu*) and peer down at their smiling faces and flowing hair reflected in its waters. As they grew older, they became self-conscious and shy of each other. In spite of this, their mutual attachment was growing stronger, and later they married. Their married life, however, was not happy. For Narihira, who was by nature passionate and fickle, soon fell in love with another woman living over the hills in Kawachi Province, to whom he paid nightly visits. But the unselfish devotion of his wife stirring his heart, he returned to her, and they lived happily together until his death. Such is the playwright's treatment of the Narihira legend where, as will be seen, the wife's love which survives her death is symbolized by the ghost that haunts the grave and offers flowers to Narihira's memory, thus suggesting the eternity of love.

In Part One a travelling priest visits a temple which, according to tradition, was built on the site of the house occupied by Narihira and his wife. The sight of an old wooden well-curb half-hidden by *susuki* grass and of an ancient tombstone, recalls to his mind their famous love-story.

In Part Two the heroine, dressed in her husband's princely robe and headgear, performs an *utsuri-mai* (impersonation dance)—in this case a type of *jo-no-mai* accompanied by a large and a small hand-drum. The climax is reached when the wife in her intense longing for the past identifies herself, as it were, with her husband and reclining on the well-curb sees his image in place of her own reflected

---

[1] Critical remarks on these poets (Abbot Henjō, Ono-no-Komachi, Bun'ya-no-Yasuhide, Ōtomo-no-Kuronushi, Monk Kisen and Ariwara-no-Narihira) appear in the preface of the *Kokinshū*.

in the still waters below her. All this, however, is but a vision. Day dawns, the vision fades, and nothing remains but dreary reality which fills the priest with sadness and regret.

Author : Zeami Motokiyo (1363–1443)

Source: *Ise Monogatari*,[1] chap. xxii; The prefatory note to the poems exchanged by the two lovers and contained in Vol. XV of the *Kokinshū*, which states explicitly that Narihira married Aritsune's daughter.

---

[1] Though the real authorship is disputed, the author of the tale is popularly attributed to Narihira himself.

IZUTSU

Persons

TRAVELLING PRIEST	*Waki*
MAIDEN	*Shite* in Part One
MAN OF THE PLACE	*Kyōgen*
GHOST OF KI-NO-ARITSUNE'S DAUGHTER	*Shite* in Part Two

Place

Ariwara Temple, Isonokami, Yamato Province

Season

Autumn

PART ONE

*Stage-attendants place on the front of the stage
a framework square well-curb with a sheaf of susuki grass at one corner.*

1

While the entrance music nanoribue *is being played,
the* PRIEST, *wearing a pointed hood, plain kimono
and broad-sleeved robe, appears and advances to the*
Shite *Seat.*

PRIEST   I am a priest on pilgrimage from province
to province. Of late I have visited the Seven
Great Temples of Nara,[1] and now am on my
way to Hatsuse.[2]

---

[1] The temples referred to are: Tōdai-ji (東大寺), Kōfuku-ji (興福寺), Gangō-ji (元興寺), Daian-ji (大
安寺), Yakushi-ji (藥師寺), Saidai-ji (西大寺), and Hōryū-ji (法隆寺). Some are situated in the city itself,
others in the neighbourhood.

Situated in Yamato Province and famous for the Hase-dera Temple dating from the eighth century.

When I enquired from someone about this temple, I was told it was the Ariwara Temple. I will enter the grounds and see what it is like.

Advances to the centre of the stage and faces the well-curb.

    Surely in bygone days the Ariwara Temple
    Was the Isonokami home
    Where Narihira and Ki-no-Aritsune's daughter
    Once lived as man and wife.
    Surely here too was written
    " Over Tatsuta's mountain pass [1]
    Perilous as storm-tossed seas. . . "

sage-uta
    As I stand on the site of this ancient tale,
    I feel the transitoriness of life.
    Now, for the sake of those twin souls,
    Will I perform religious rites,
    Will I perform religious rites.

Joins his hands in prayer and moves to the Waki *Seat.*

2

While the entrance music shidai *is being played, the* MAIDEN, *wearing a 'young woman' mask, wig, painted gold-patterned under-kimono and brocade outer-kimono, appears carrying a spray of leaves [2] and stands at the* Shite *Seat.*

MAIDEN
shidai
    Gazing into the crystal water I draw each morning,

---

[1] Pass crossing a hill of the same name in the mountain-range between Yamato and Kawachi Provinces. The Tatsuta Shrine, one of the most ancient Shinto temples, situated on the eastern slope of Tatsuta Hill south of Mt. Shigi, was erected in the seventh century by Imperial order and dedicated to the wind-god. The river flowing east of the hill is also called Tatsuta and has been much celebrated in ancient literature on account of the autumn tints of the maples which line its banks.

[2] Or a small wooden bucket with a spray of leaves representing flowers.

Gazing into the crystal water I draw each
morning,

The moon, too, seems to cleanse her heart.

CHORUS   Gazing into the crystal water I draw each
jidori   morning,

The moon, too, seems to cleanse her heart.

MAIDEN   Autumn nights are lonely anywhere,
sashi   Yet even lonelier

Is this old temple rarely visited,

When the autumn winds sough through the
garden pines.

The moon sinking westward,

The drooping eaves o'ergrown with waving
ferns—

All reminds me of the past.

Alas! how long must I still live

And naught to hope for in the future!

Each thing that happens leaves its mark
upon the mind;

Such is our mortal world.

sage-uta   Buddha, I cast myself on thee

With all my heart, praying continually

That with the unseen thread held in thy
hand[1]

Thou wilt at last lead me to Paradise!

age-uta   Thy vow is to enlighten those in darkness,

Thy vow is to enlighten those in darkness.

Although the moon at dawn

Does surely hasten towards the western
hills

---

[1] In Jōdo-kyō except for the Shin sect, it was customary for a dying person to hold in the left hand one end of a thread attached to a hand of the image of Amida Buddha in order that he should fix his mind on His saving power.

Where lies the Land of Bliss,
Yet between here and there
Stretches the vast and empty autumn sky
As far as eye can reach.
We hear the winds soughing through the
    pines,
But know not whence they blow nor
    whither.[1]

In this world more fleeting than the wind, *Comes to the front of the stage, sits down, places the spray of leaves before her and joins her hands in prayer, then returns to the Shite Seat.*
Vain dreams deceive our minds.
What call will have the power to waken us,
What call will have the power to waken us!

3

PRIEST   While meditating in the temple grounds I see   *Turns to the MAIDEN.*
an attractive woman draw water from a well
with a wooden curb and, having poured it into
a wooden vessel containing flowers, offer it
reverently to a grass-covered
mound.   Pray,   who   are
you?

MAIDEN   I   am   a   woman   of   this
neighbourhood.   The   pious
benefactor   of   this   temple,
Ariwara-no-Narihira, was a famous man and
the tombstone by this mound is supposed to be
his.   Therefore I offer flowers to it and pray
for his salvation.

PRIEST   Yes, Narihira has left an undying name behind him.   This place may indeed have been

---

[1] The metaphor seems analogous to that found in the third chapter of *St. John*, except that here
the changeableness of wind is used to symbolize the uncertainty of human life.

the site of his home, but since his story goes back to ancient times, I am filled with wonder that any one, especially a woman, should thus be praying for him.

Perchance you are related to him?

MAIDEN   You ask whether I am related to him? But even in his day he was called the 'Ancient.'[1] Now, after this long lapse of time, he belongs to the remote past. How can there still live any one related to him?

PRIEST   You speak truth,
Yet this was once his home.
MAIDEN   Though he is long since dead,
PRIEST   This place remains as it was once,
MAIDEN   And tales that keep his fame alive
PRIEST   Are handed down to us.
MAIDEN   So the 'Ancient'
CHORUS   Is still remembered,
age-uta   Though time-worn is the Ariwara Temple,
Though time-worn is the Ariwara Temple.
Grass covers this mound
Shadowed by ancient pines,
And only this one bush
Of flowering susuki
Marks where he sleeps for evermore,
And might, indeed, unfold a tale
Of bygone days.
The sight of this old mound,
Hidden under lush grass
Drenched with weary dew,

[1] Each chapter of the Ise Monogatari begins with the words: "In ancient times there was a man." Since the anonymous hero is understood to be Narihira, the author of the present play pretends that Narihira was called the 'Ancient' in his life-time.

Is precious to the lonely heart,
Is precious to the lonely heart !

The MAIDEN *sits down and weeps.*

4

PRIEST   I wish you would tell me more about Narihira.

The MAIDEN *rises and, coming to the centre of the stage, sits down.*

CHORUS
kuri   Once Narihira, captain of the Imperial
Body-guard,
Enjoyed for many years spring flowers and
autumn moons
Here at Isonokami, then fallen into decay.

MAIDEN
sashi   'Twas when he lived in wedlock
With Ki-no-Aritsune's daughter,
Bound each to other by strong love !

CHORUS   Later bewitched by a new love
At Takayasu[1] in Kawachi Province,
And loth to give up either,
Secretly he visited her of nights.

MAIDEN   " Over Tatsuta's mountain pass,
CHORUS   Perilous as storm-tossed seas,
He speeds at midnight all alone ! "
Thus sang his wife
Fearing that treacherous pass.
Moved by her selfless love,
His new love withered.

MAIDEN   Since poetry alone can tell our deepest
feelings,

CHORUS   Well might her selfless love inspire such a
moving poem.

kuse   Here in this province long ago
Two households once lived side by side,

1 Situated at the foot of a mountain of the same name in Naka-Kawachi County of that province.

The children, boy and girl, were playmates;
Leaning over the well-curb beyond the gate,
They peered together down the well
Where mirrored lay their faces cheek to
    cheek,
Their sleeves hanging o'er each other's
    shoulder.
Thus used those bosom friends to play.
In time they grew reserved and shy,
Till the faithful-hearted youth
Sent her a letter with a poem
Telling his flower-like love
In words like sparkling dew-drops:

MAIDEN   " Standing against the well-curb,
As children we compared our heights,
CHORUS   But I have grown much taller
Since last I saw you."[1]
Answering the maiden wrote:
" The hair I parted
When by the well-curb we compared
    our heights,
Now loose flows down my back.
For whom but you should it again be
    tied? "[2]
For this exchange of poems
They called her the 'Lady of the Well-
    Curb.'

5

CHORUS   Listening to this ancient lovers' tale,
rongi   I am filled with wonder at your charm.

[1,2] Quoted from the *Ise Monogatari*, chap. xxii.

Please disclose your name !

MAIDEN   If you would know the truth,
Taking the shape of Aritsune's daughter,
By yearning moved, I have come back to
my old home,
Treading under the veil of night
A road perilous as the Tatsuta Pass.

CHORUS   How wonderful !
Then you are the lady of the Tatsuta Pass?

MAIDEN   " Daughter of Ki-no-Aritsune " am I

CHORUS   And " Lady of the Well-Curb " too.

MAIDEN   With shame I own to both those names.

CHORUS   Scarce has she revealed the name
Of her who tied the nuptial knot
When but nineteen
And made her vow before the gods,
Than she fades away behind the well-curb,
Than she fades away behind the well-curb.

The MAIDEN *rises.*

The MAIDEN *goes out.*

INTERLUDE

The MAN OF THE PLACE *enters the stage,
wearing a striped kimono, sleeveless robe and trailing
divided skirt, and short sword. In reply to the*
PRIEST's *request, he tells him the tale of* Ki-no-Aritsune's DAUGHTER.

PART TWO

1

PRIEST   The night is growing old !

machi-utai   Above the temple hangs the moon,
Above the temple hangs the moon.

Wishing to dream of times gone by,
I turn my robe inside out,[1]
And lay me down upon this bed of moss,
And lay me down upon this bed of moss.

2

While the entrance music issei *is being played, the*
GHOST OF KI-NO-ARITSUNE'S DAUGHTER, *wearing
a 'young woman' mask, wig, man's ceremonial
headgear, painted gold-patterned under-kimono, dancing*
chōken *robe and embroidered* koshimaki *outer-
kimono, appears and stands at the* Shite *Seat.*

DAUGHTER
sashi

" Though people call them shifty,
Yet the cherry-blossoms never fail
Him who seeks my garden once a year
Less for my sake than for theirs. '[2]
This poem gained for me
The name of ' Friend-Awaiting Woman.'
Many a year has passed with varying for-
tunes
Since Narihira and I played by the well-
curb ;
Now bereft of him, though ill-becoming,
I don this robe he gave me
And dance as he was wont to do.

CHORUS

Graceful as whirling flakes of snow,

---

[1] It was an ancient custom for overs to sleep with their kimono turned inside out so that they
might dream of their belovèd, as mentioned in a poem by Ono-no-Komachi in the *Kokinshū* :

> When overwhelmed
> By the yearning for the one I love,
> I go to bed,
> Wearing my garment inside out.

[2] Quoted from the *Ise Monogatari*, chap. xvi, as attributed to the hero of the work, i.e. Narihira.
The poem is also found in the *Kokinshū* where the author's name is not mentioned.

The dancer waves her flowery sleeves.
The DAUGHTER *performs a* jo-no-mai *dance.*

DAUGHTER Hither returned I call back time past
CHORUS   And on the ancient well
          Of the Ariwara Temple
          The moon shines brightly as of old,
          The moon shines brightly as of old.

3

DAUGHTER " Is not the moon in heaven the same ?
          Is not the springtime as it was ? "[1]
          Thus did he sing, long, long ago.
          " Standing against the well-curb,
CHORUS   Standing against the well-curb,
          As children we compared our heights.
DAUGHTER But I
CHORUS   Have grown much taller."
DAUGHTER And much older.
CHORUS   Wearing this robe and headgear
          As Narihira did,
          It does not look like a woman,
          But a man—the living image of Narihira.
DAUGHTER How dear the face I see !
CHORUS   How dear the face, though it be mine !
          See ! The ghost of the dead lady fades
          Like the lingering scent of fading flowers.
          The sky is turning grey ;
          The Ariwara Temple's bell starts to toll,
          Ushering in the morn.
          The garden pines awaken with the breeze ;

*Dances while the fol-
lowing lines are chanted.*

*Approaching the well,
the* DAUGHTER *pushes
aside the* susuki *grass
and peers down into it.*

The DAUGHTER
moves away.

*She wraps the left
sleeve round her arm
and covers her face with
the open fan and bends
forward.*

*She stands still as if
listening to the bel!.*

---

[1] Quoted from the *Ise Monogatari*, chap. iv. The poem, which also appears in the *Kokinshū* and is a cry of a heart-broken lover whose beloved had been taken away whither he did not know, is translated in its full form on p. 83, note 1.

And like the torn leaves of the *bashō*[1]-tree
The priest's dream is shattered and day
    dawns,
The priest's dream is shattered and day
    dawns.

                 She stamps twice at
                 the Shite *Seat.*

[1] See *Bashō,* p. 127, note 1.

105

EGUCHI

EGUCHI

LADY   I own to be the Lady of Eguchi, for so I
      once was called
And this, most reverend sir, a moon-view-
      ing party.
                    —Part II, scene 2.

INTRODUCTION

Eguchi is a typical *kazura-mono* or 'female wig' play. It belongs to the subdivision called *daishō-jo-no-mai-mono* which has a special dance accompanied by a large and a small hand-drum as well as a flute.

In olden days the town of Eguchi[1] on the river Yodo in Settsu Province was a pleasure resort famous for the courtesans it provided for the entertainment of travellers. The most celebrated of these was known as the " Lady of Eguchi." According to tradition Saigyō (1118–90), the hermit poet, finding himself benighted at Eguchi, asked her for a night's lodging, but was refused, whereupon he composed and recited the lines,

> "Yet even for one night
> You grudge me your temporary lodging."[2]

The truth, however, was that the Lady of Eguchi did not really grudge giving him shelter, but only refused his request for the good of his soul. Wishing that he should rise above caring for such earthly things, she riposted with the lines,

> "I would you took no thought
> For a temporary lodging."[3]

According to another tradition,[4] the courtesan who made this ready repartee, was an incarnation of Fugen[5] Bosatsu (Bodhisattva Samantabhadra). The theme of the present play is derived from a combination of these two traditions.

Part One tells how a travelling monk and his two attendants on their way from Miyako to the Tennō-ji Temple[6] in Osaka, arrived at Eguchi. Remembering the legend of the Lady of Eguchi, he asks to be directed to the site of her ancient

---

[1] Name of one of the fords across the river Yodo (see p. 114, note 1.), formerly the estuary of that river ; hence its name " River-mouth." In the Heian period it was a very flourishing sea-port town where sea-going ships carrying passengers and merchandise bound for Miyako transhipped their cargoes to river-boats. It was also much famed for its brothels and the beauty of their inmates.

[2,3] Poems contained in Saigyō's *Senjūshō*.

[4] Referred to in the *Jikkinshō*, where the heroine is a courtesan of Kwanzaki, Settsu Province, instead of the Lady of Eguchi.

[5] Fugen and Monju are two great Bodhisattvas of the Buddha triad who assist Sakyamuni in the work of salvation. The former is represented sitting on a white elephant which symbolizes the majestic self-possession and mighty power the Bodhisattva attained through meditation and spiritual training.

[6] Large Buddhist temple in Osaka founded in the sixth century by Prince-Regent Shōtoku.

home, which inspires him to recite Saigyō's poem. No sooner has he done so than her ghost suddenly appears and, after explaining the real motive for refusing Saigyō a night's lodging, vanishes.

In the Interlude the mystified monk then asks his guide to tell him about the Lady of Eguchi and learns that local tradition credits her with being an incarnation of Bodhisattva Fugen. An ancient legend[1] also tells how Shōkū Shōnin (910–1007) of Mt. Shosha in Harima Province prayed earnestly to Kwannon Bosatsu (Bodhisattva Avalokiteshvara) to let him see Fugen in visible form.

One night, in a dream, he was told to go to Eguchi in Settsu Province and to seek out the courtesan known as the Lady of Eguchi. On reaching the place he found her in a boat on the river with other courtesans making merry. As the Shōnin closed his eyes, the murmuring waters seemed like voices sweetly chanting verses from the Holy Sutra. Suddenly the glorious vision of Bodhisattva Fugen attended by a host of female *rasetsu*[2] appeared before him, and he knew that his prayer had been answered. When again he opened his eyes there was the Lady of Eguchi in her human form as before. So deeply moved was the monk by the tale told him by the Man of the Place that he agreed to recite sutras in her honour.

Part Two represents the vision of the Lady of Eguchi which appears to the chanting monks. A gay framework barge is brought on to the Bridgeway in which the Lady and two young women are standing in the gorgeous attire of courtesans. Charming songs and graceful dances appropriate to such a river party are performed. The songs express the religious truth that the world is only a temporary sojourn and that when one attains spiritual detachment from the world, the transient will be found to be the eternal, and passion and wisdom to be one. The heroine who cries, " Oh, rapture ! " and is inspired by the revelation to perform a dance, is no longer a mere courtesan and, at the end, transformed into Bodhisattva Fugen riding a milk-white elephant, is borne away on a cloud. Gazing at this, the monk sheds tears of heavenly joy.

Eguchi technically occupies a very high place among Noh plays on account of the interesting and very difficult double role of the heroine, at once a beautiful and witty courtesan and Bodhisattva Fugen, and illustrates the Mahayana

---

[1] The author deliberately grafts the legend of Shōkū Shōnin and the courtesan of Kwanzaki on to the tale of the Lady of Eguchi, thus preparing for the later revelation of the identity of the Eguchi courtesan and the Bodhisattva Fugen.

[2] *Rasetsu* or *rakshasi* are beautiful man-eating she-devils who, according to the *Lotus Sutra*, vowed ever to protect all believers in the power of the Sutra during the third Buddhist evil millennium when Buddhism decays.

doctrine that even the meanest creature in the world is potentially a Bodhisattva, thus explaining the apparent contradiction between the two personalities.

Author: Kwannami Kiyotsugu (1334–1384)

Source: *Shin Kokinshū* (1205), *Jikkinshō* (1252), *Kojidan* (1212–1215), and *Senjūshō* (1183).

EGUCHI

Persons

TRAVELLING MONK	*Waki*
TWO ATTENDANTS	*Waki-zure*
MAN OF THE PLACE	*Kyōgen*
WOMAN	*Shite* in Part One
GHOST OF LADY OF EGUCHI	*Shite* in Part Two
TWO WOMEN ATTENDANTS	*Tsure*

Place

Town of Eguchi, Settsu Province

Season

Autumn

PART ONE

1

While the entrance music shidai *is being played,
the* TRAVELLING MONK *and* TWO ATTENDANTS
*enter the stage. They are wearing pointed hoods,
small-checked under-kimonos, white broad
divided skirts and broad-sleeved robes.*

MONK and ATTENDANTS

shidai   If the moon is an old friend,

      If the moon is an old friend,

      How can we flee the world?[1]

[1] The meaning of the two lines is: " We have, indeed, renounced the world, in the popular sense
of the term, but when we look at the moon or at other natural objects, we find it is an old friend. Thus,

113

CHORUS   If the moon is an old friend,
jidori   How can we flee the world?
MONK   I am a monk travelling from province to prov-
              ince.   Since I have not yet visited the Tennō-ji
              Temple in Settsu Province, I have decided to
              make a pilgrimage to that holy shrine.

MONK and ATTENDANTS
michi-yuki   Leaving Miyako before dawn,
              We take boat down the river Yodo[1];
              We pass reedy Udono[2];
              Then in the hazy distance we sight
              Eguchi's clustering pines and lapping waves,
              And at long last we reach the town itself,
              And at long last we reach the town itself.

MONK   Is any inhabitant of Eguchi about?

              The MAN OF THE PLACE, *wearing a striped kimono,*
              sleeveless robe and trailing divided skirt, rises from
              the Kyōgen *Seat and moves to the First Pine.*

MAN   You are asking for someone of this place.   *The* ATTENDANTS
              What is your pleasure?   *sit in front of the*
                                              CHORUS, *while the*
MONK   I am a monk from Miyako here for the first   MONK *stands at the*
              time.   Please direct me to the spot where the   Shite *Seat.*
              Lady of Eguchi lived in ancient times.

MAN   It is over there.   You are welcome to go and
              see it, if you care to.

MONK   Thank you for your kindness.   I shall go there
              and see what there is to be seen.

strictly speaking, nature is also part of the world ; how then can one get outside it? " These words seem to
adumbrate a dualistic way of thinking to be refuted by the Bodhisattva's revelation at the close of the play.
    [1] The rivers Uji and Katsura join at the town of Yodo, south of Kyoto, and form the river Yodo
which is navigable and flows into the Bay of Osaka. The town was the starting-point for river-boats
plying between there and Osaka.
    [2] Place on the river Yodo famed for its lush growth of reeds.

MAN	If you need anything further, I shall be at your service.
MONK	Thank you.

The MAN *sits on the* Kyōgen *Seat.*

2

MONK *sashi*	Is this where the Lady of Eguchi lived?

Stands at the centre of the stage.

> Though her body, alas! long since rests buried in the earth,
> Her memory is for ever green.

'Tis sad to view the scene of the ancient tale.

It is said that in days gone by the monk Saigyō came here and asked for a night's lodging, but the lady of the house refused him, and he composed the poem:

> Hard may it be for you, a woman,
> To cast the world far from you,
> Yet even for one night
> You grudge me your temporary lodging.

It must have been just here.

Alas, poor soul!

Oh! . . . Reverend sir!

Voice of a woman behind the Curtain.

The WOMAN *enters, wearing a 'young woman' mask, painted gold-patterned under-kimono and brocade outer-kimono.*

WOMAN	Oh! What prompted you to recite that poem?
MONK	How strange that a woman should appear when there are no houses to be seen, and ask why I recited the poem! But what is that to you?
WOMAN	I had long forgotten it, but that poem has brought it all back to me.

Though the world is like dew on the
  grassy plain,
To renounce it may be too hard for a woman,
But worse than that, I denied a traveller
Even a lodging for the night.
Thus says the poem to my shame.
But since I did not mean what those words   *Advances singing on*
  implied,   *to the stage.*
I now have come to tell you why I did so.

MONK   I cannot understand. Finding myself on the
spot where long ago Saigyō said,
  " Yet even for one night
  You grudge me your temporary lodging,"[1]
I have been feeling vaguely
sorry for the lady of the house.
And now you appear and say you
did not grudge him shelter, as we
have supposed.

  Who may you be?

WOMAN   Stay ! It is just as I had guessed. Why did
you not also recite my poem, which shows I
did not really grudge it?

MONK   Yes, I remember :
  " Since I am told you are a monk,

WOMAN   Who has renounced the world,
  I would you took no thought
  For a temporary lodging."[2]
  So I advised him. Had I not good reason to
refuse him lodging in such a house?

MONK   Yes, you were right,
  Since Saigyō had renounced this worldly life,

[1,2] See p. 109, note 2. This poetic dialogue is also given in the *Shin Kokinshū*, where the authorship of the latter poem is attributed to a lady called Tae.

WOMAN	And ours was a notorious house of pleasure with many mysteries.
	In such a place
MONK	You said he should not seek a lodging,
WOMAN	Being mindful of his holy life.
MONK	Yet people say
WOMAN	I grudged him shelter.
CHORUS	To grudge
age-uta	In such a case is not to grudge,
	In such a case is not to grudge.
	Why should folk say that I was grudging?
	That ancient story has been handed down,
	But, reverend sir, heed not that idle tale.

3

CHORUS	Dusk is falling as I listen to the well-known
rongi	story.
	Who is she who before my eyes
	Now grows dim and shadow-like?
WOMAN	The figure standing in the dusk
	May seem to you the Lady of Eguchi,
	Who lived a life of ill repute,
	By a half-hidden creek along this river.
	O shame!
CHORUS	And surely in this place she passed away
	Like a spent wave upon the beach.
WOMAN	" The flowering plum-tree
CHORUS	At my house of sojourn
	Maybe has caught your eye,
WOMAN	Since unlooked-for
CHORUS	You have come."[1]

[1] Poem by Taira-no-Kanemori contained in the *Shūishū* (*c.* 1000). The ghost quotes the poem to express her joy at the monk's unexpected visit to the site of her former house.

117

Nay, but your coming here
Originates from some bond in our previous
   lives,
Were it no more
Than taking shelter under the same tree,
Or drawing water from the same stream.[1]
Of this you can be sure !
I am the Lady of Eguchi's ghost ! . . .
Saying these words she fades away,
Saying these words she fades away.

Goes out.

INTERLUDE

The MONK *again calls the* MAN OF THE PLACE, *who tells him of a legend according to which the* LADY OF EGUCHI *was an incarnation of Fugen Bosatsu. He then mentions to him the apparition of the* WOMAN, *with whom he has just conversed. At his suggestion the* MONK *prepares to chant some sutra in her honour.*

PART TWO

1

MONK   The Lady of Eguchi must have assumed a visible form in order to speak with me.

     Now, let us chant a requiem for her ghost.

MONK and ATTENDANTS

machi-utai   I had no sooner finished speaking, than, behold !
     I had no sooner finished speaking, than, behold !

---

[1] See *Tamura*, p. 32, note 1.

There on the shimmering river waters
A pleasure-boat with singing courtesans
Appeared floating in the moonlight. A
    wondrous sight !
Appeared floating in the moonlight. A
    wondrous sight !

2

*A framework barge is placed on the Bridgeway.
While the entrance music* issei *is being played, the*
Lady of Eguchi *enters the barge. She wears the
same mask as in Part One, brocade outer-kimono
tucked up, and scarlet broad divided skirt.* Two
Women Attendants *follow her, wearing* tsure
*masks, painted gold-patterned under-kimonos and brocade
outer-kimonos. One of them carries a bamboo pole
and has her right arm slipped out of her outer-kimono.*

Chorus	Mooring our barge,
age-uta	Rocked gently by the waves we meet our lovers,

Rocked gently by the waves we meet our
    lovers.
Lured by the empty dreams of life,
Alas ! we know not our true state.
Our sleeves are wet with tears like
    Lady Sayo[1]
Who, from a hill above Matsura,
Followed with tear-dimmed eyes

[1] In 537 when Mimana (任那) in Korea, then a tributary of Japan, was invaded by a neighbouring state, the Emperor Senka sent Ōtomo-no-Sadehiko with troops to relieve the country. His wife Sayo-hime accompanied him as far as Matsura, Hizen Province, Kyūshū. As his ship was setting sail, she climbed a hill near-by shedding bitter tears and waving her scarf, and refused to leave even after the ship was lost to sight. So heart-breaking were her lamentations that a legend later arose to the effect that Lady Sayo was turned into a stone, which is still standing on the hill.

119

The ship that bore her lord to far Korea.
We, too, like the Lady of Uji Bridge,[1]
Have known the bitterness
Of vainly watching, waiting
For the return of a faithless lover.
Be that as it may, this world is good,
Be that as it may, this world is good,
With its flowers and snows, its waves and
    clouds !
May prosperity attend us in this life !

MONK   O wondrous sight !
Lo ! upon the moonlit waters
A flock of luring courtesans
Are singing gaily.
Whose barge is it, I wonder?

LADY   Whose barge, you ask?
I own to be the Lady of Eguchi, for so I
    once was called,
And this, most reverend sir, a moon-view-
    ing party.

MONK   You call yourself the Lady of Eguchi,
The same as she of olden days?

LADY   Say not " of olden days." Look at the moon !
Has she changed since olden days?

ATTENDANTS See ! Are we not here too?
To say that we belong to olden days is silly !

LADY   If you have more to say or ask,

ATTENDANTS We shall not listen or reply.

---

[1] Alludes to an anonymous poem in the *Kokinshū*, which reads :
> Lying dressed on her sleeping mat,
> This night too
> She must be waiting for me,
> O poor Lady of Uji Bridge !

Scholars have not yet discovered the lady's identity.

LADY	How vexing !
LADY and ATTENDANTS	
issei	" The autumn waters flow swift and deep ;
	The boat darts down the stream,"[1]
LADY	Merrily sing the girls,
	Their oars glitter in the moonlight.
CHORUS	Come ! Let us sing away the night !
sage-uta	We are ladies of pleasure in a boat,
	Stirred by yearning for the past;
	Let us seek easement in those ancient
	ditties
	We once did sing to charm our guests.

3

CHORUS	" The Law of the Twelve Causes[2] is like
kuri	unto a wheel
	Endlessly rolling along a highway;
LADY	Sentient creatures now sink, now rise,
	Like birds that fly from branch to branch."[3]
CHORUS	Life after life into the past—
LADY	Whence the cycle first began is hidden from
	us.
CHORUS	Life after life into the future—
	Whither the cycle ends we cannot know.
LADY	Sometimes creatures are born into the happy
sashi	state

The LADY *and the* ATTENDANTS *step out of the barge, which is removed. Advancing to the centre of the stage, she sits on a stool while the others sit in front of the Flute-player.*

---

[1] First line of a Chinese couplet contained in the *Wakan Rōeishū*. The second line reads :
    The clouds of night have vanished
    And the moon is sailing slowly across the sky.
[2] Buddhist doctrine which explains the workings of *karma* as the principle of existence. The Twelve Causes are twelve links in the endless chain of lives and deaths and, according to one interpretation, give rise to past, present and future lives. They are : ignorance and activity (in the past life) : consciousness, the foetal senses, the six organs of perception, sensation and discrimination, choice, pursuit, *karma* (in the present life) : birth and death (in the future life).
[3] Quotation from the *Rokudō Kōshiki.*

121

Of men or heavenly beings,

CHORUS Yet by error overcast, their minds

Fail to sow the seed of salvation;

LADY Sometimes they're reborn into the Three
Worst States,[1]

Or fall a prey to the Eight Evils,[2]

CHORUS And fettered by such misfortunes

They know not how to enter the True Way.[3]

LADY And we, though born in human form—

A chance that rarely comes to pass—

CHORUS Were born frail vessels of sin;

Most helpless of all women, like reeds
carried down the stream.[4]

Grievous it is to think upon the sins

Committed by us in our former lives.

kuse On spring mornings

The hills do clothe themselves in pink-
brocade robes

Which evening breezes scatter;

On autumn evenings

Tinted leaves dapple the trees with gold,

Only to wither under the morning frost.

Fanned by the breezes through the pines,

Or lit up by the creeper-veiled moon,

The LADY rises and dances while the following lines are chanted.

---

[1] Buddhism teaches that an unenlightened soul is eternally bound by its *karma* to wander about the six states of existence, i.e. the world of heavenly beings, of human beings, of Asuras, of hungry devils, of brutes and of hell; of these states the first three are the best and the last three the worst.

[2] What is common to the Eight Evils is that those subject to them cannot see buddhas or hear the right way and that they are due to the nature of the conditions in which souls find themselves. If a soul is an inhabitant of hell, or a brute or a hungry devil it is unable, because of its sufferings, to listen to the preaching of the Law; if it is born in the 'heaven of long life' or according to ancient Indian cosmography, in the northern continent of Uttan-otsu, it cannot become an earnest believer in the Law because it enjoys longevity. One who is born blind, deaf or dumb, or is too worldly-wise or sophisticated cannot believe in the Way. Finally one who is born before or after the time of a buddha, will find great difficulty in attaining faith in his teachings.

[3] Some sects of Buddhism hold that the gate of salvation is closed to women, so that it is necessary for them to be transformed into men before being able to attain Buddhahood.

[4] Metaphor for the career of a harlot.

The guests we spoke to face to face
Leave us, never to return.
Lovers whose pillows lie side by side
Under green curtains in red bowers,
In time grow cold.
Can any creature—insentient plant or sentient man—
Escape from mutability?
Yet though we know this,

LADY   Lured by the eye
We grow attached to things;

CHORUS   Ravished by sweet sounds
We become their thralls.
Such things deceive the mind
And lead the tongue to falseness.
Alas! Man is a wanderer in the world of
the Six Dusts
And sins through the Six Organs of Perception,
Yet most temptations come through the eye
and the ear.

4

CHORUS   O rapture!

The LADY *performs a* jo-no-mai *dance.*

5

LADY   The boundless ocean of Reality and Truth   *Continues to dance*
Is never ruffled by the winds   *while the following*
Of the Five Defilements[1] and the Six *lines are chanted.*
Desires,[2]

---

[1] See *Tamura*, p. 25, note 5.
[2] I.e. six desires for the pleasing objects perceived through the five senses and the mind.

CHORUS	And yet the waves of Moving-Being[1]
	Day in, day out, do rise,
	Day in, day out, do rise.
LADY	What causes these waves to rise?
	Man's vain attachment
	To his temporary lodging.
CHORUS	But once man has attained detachment,
	The fleeting world exists no more;
LADY	Lovers no longer
CHORUS	Are anxiously waited for when night falls;
LADY	No more the grief of parting.
CHORUS	Spring flowers and autumn leaves,
	Moon and snow—all cease to move him.
LADY	I recall to mind,
CHORUS	" I recall to mind
	I told one to take no thought
	For a temporary lodging.
	Adieu, monk ! I must return."

See ! Bodhisattva Fugen now reveals herself,

The barge becomes a milk-white elephant,

And aureoled Fugen sails,

Borne by snow-white clouds,

Across the western sky.

Oh ! gracious vision, flooding the heart with
joy,

Oh ! gracious vision, flooding the heart with
joy !

*Advancing to the
centre of the stage, the
LADY pauses and
stamps repeatedly,
thereby symbolizing her
ascension.*

*She stamps twice at
the Shite Seat.*

---

[1] Moving-Being is another way of saying ' Reality subject to causation (隨緣眞如) as contrasted
with Immutable Reality (不變眞如) '; both are aspects of reality which expresses itself in phenomena
while retaining its substance unchanged and undefiled.

BASHŌ

CHORUS   Its sleeves are sadly torn.
What a disgrace!
—Part II, scene 3.

INTRODUCTION

Bashō is a *kazura-mono* or 'female wig' play in which the *jo-no-mai* dance is performed without the accompaniment of a horizontal drum.

Inspired by the Buddhist doctrine that plants can attain Buddhahood, the author personifies the *bashō*-tree [1] as a pensive woman who, in the presence of a hermit renowned for his saintliness, expresses in impassioned words her feeling of gratitude towards this Buddhist doctrine explained in the " Parable of the Medicinal Plants " in the *Lotus Sutra*. The beneficent influence of rain and dew, though but simple water, causes all manner of plants to grow and blossom, thus illustrating Buddha's teaching that all creatures in the universe may be led to develop their inherent Buddha-nature. But since ineffable Absolute Reality is the fundamental nature of all beings, everything that exists is identified with the Absolute. All things, while they are subject, individually, to birth and death and are finite both as to attributes and functions, constitute an organic whole ; they intermingle and interact by virtue of the oneness of their nature, thus constituting a single life. The latter is ever-growing and changing, yet may, at any moment, return to the one reality which transcends existence and non-existence, i.e. to the ineffable Absolute.

Buddhist enlightenment consists in the realization of the oneness of all things. And since all creatures are endowed with Buddha-nature, all may attain enlightenment, which is but another way of saying that they can become Buddhas. Everything, therefore, whether sentient or non-sentient, is held capable of reverting to ultimate reality, if given the opportunity. From this point of view the *bashō*-tree, for instance, may also attain Buddhahood. The salvation of a plant, however, is not a privilege limited to this individual plant. That a *bashō*-tree, as in the case of the heroine of the present play, should have attained Buddhahood is a proof that all other trees of the same kind, and indeed, the whole of plant life, are destined to achieve the same blessedness by virtue of the all-pervading oneness of nature.

The scene is laid in ancient China by a river in the land of Tsu. A *bashō*-tree growing nearby happens to hear a hermit reciting the *Lotus Sutra*. The sacred

---

[1] *Musa Basjoo*, a banana-like plant with large leaves found in southern Japan.

words give it the chance of gaining enlightenment and, ultimately, Buddhahood. Since dramatic requirements demand, however, that the tree should assume a form suitable for presentation on the stage, it is represented in human shape. The *bashō*-tree with its soft straight stem crowned with large, glossy leaves seems to possess certain feminine characteristics, but, lacking attractiveness, it is represented as a woman past her prime. Again, since the *bashō* is originally an exotic plant, though found in parts of the mainland of Japan, this may have led the author to place the scene of the play in China. It should further be noted that in Buddhist literature the *bashō*-tree is a symbol of impermanence and as such tends to evoke feelings of melancholy.

A hermit who has embraced a particularly rigorous rule of life, while in mid-autumn reciting nightly aloud the *Lotus Sutra*, becomes aware of the presence of some one in the moonlit garden outside his cell-window. Upon enquiring who it is, a woman confesses that she is the spirit of a *bashō*-tree. In token of her gratitude for the opportunity afforded her to gain enlightenment through listening to the reading of the *Lotus Sutra*, she performs a dance, waving her sleeves which represent the broad leaves of the *bashō*-tree.

Such is the story of the play which, as will be seen, has practically no plot. Apart from illustrating the doctrine of the universal Buddha-nature, its chief interest lies in the graceful dance by an elderly woman clad in ' robe of ice ' and ' skirt of frost ' designed to awaken chaste emotions in the hearts of the audience.

Author : Komparu-Zenchiku (1405–1468)

Source : *Hu-hai-hsin-wen* (湖海新聞), which contains the anecdote of a *bashō*-tree disguised as a woman visiting a hermit; and the " Parable of the Medicinal Plants " in the *Lotus Sutra*, which gave rise to the doctrine concerning the attainment of Buddhahood by plants.

BASHŌ

Persons

HERMIT LIVING AMONG THE HILLS	*Waki*
WOMAN	*Shite* in Part One
MAN OF THE PLACE	*Kyōgen*
SPIRIT OF A BASHŌ-TREE	*Shite* in Part Two

Place

Hermitage near the River Hsiang-hsui in the Land of Tsu, China

Season

Autumn

PART ONE

1

While the entrance music nanoribue *is being played, the* Hermit, *wearing a pointed hood, striped kimono, broad-sleeved robe, appears and advances to the* Shite Seat *with a sutra scroll slipped into the opening of his kimono.*

HERMIT   I am a monk who lives among the hills near the River Shōsui[1] in the Land of So in China. As I am a believer in the *Lotus Sutra*, I chant it aloud morning and evening, day and night.

---

[1] I.e. Hsiang-hsui (湘水). 'So' is the Japanese for 'Tsu.'

129

More than ever now that it is mid-autumn and the bright moon shines in the sky, I never relax my nightly devotions.

Now here is something strange: though no one lives in these deserted hills save myself, yet night after night while I am reciting the sutra, I hear someone outside my hermit's cell. If he should come again to-night, I think I will ask his name.

Goes to the Waki *Seat and sits down.*

sashi
    Already the evening sun is setting in the west,
    Shadows deepen in the valleys,
    The cries of homing birds grow faint.

age-uta
    Slowly the night fills with radiance,
    Slowly the night fills with radiance,
    And as the autumn moon climbs to the sky,
    In the stillness of my cell
    Buried in the heart of the hills,
    I read aloud the sacred book,
    I read aloud the sacred book.

2

While the entrance music shidai *is being played, the* WOMAN *appears and advances to the* Shite *Seat. She wears a* Fukai *mask, wig, painted gold-patterned under-kimono, and 'not-red' brocade outer-kimono and carries a rosary of crystal beads in the right hand and a spray of leaves in the left.*

WOMAN
shidai
    The wind sweeps downwards through the pines,
    The wind sweeps downwards through the pines,

	Wantonly breaking the *bashō* leaves.
CHORUS *jidori*	The wind sweeps downwards through the pines,
	Wantonly breaking the *bashō* leaves.
WOMAN *sashi*	" Through the broken window
	The gusts will blow out the lamp ;
	Piercing the ill-thatched roof
	The moon-beams chase sleep from my eyes."[1]

Thus must I spend the autumn nights,

Lost in the depths of these deserted hills ;

Who is there to know my plight?

And thus my withered life draws to its close.

sage-uta	For such a lonely one as I
	Can have no friend save rocks and trees.
age-uta	'Tis hard to meet

The *Lotus Sutra*, and profound its truth,

The *Lotus Sutra*, and profound its truth.

Unless its spirit fill their hearts,

Even though clad in rich brocade,

Men cannot gain that peerless gem[2]

That will light up their minds.

My rugged sleeves are wet with dew and tears,

Takes two or three steps forward and, sitting down, places the spray of leaves on the

---

[1] Quotation from a poem by Tu Sun-he (杜荀鶴) of the T'ang dynasty.

[2] Allusion to a parable in the " Book of the Five Hundred Disciples Receiving Buddha's Testimonial concerning their Future Buddhahood (第百弟子受記品) " in the *Lotus Sutra*. The parable tells how a man who was being entertained at a friend's house got drunk and fell asleep. Being called away to a remote country on urgent public business, before his departure, he sewed a priceless gem into the lining of his friend's garment. The latter also went off to another country and, having become very poor, had to earn his living by doing manual labour. After many years the friends met. Seeing his wretched condition, he told the latter about the gem which was still in the lining of his garment and that, had his friend only known, it would have saved him from all his misery. The gem is a symbol of the Buddha-nature found in every creature.

131

The months and years will come and go,

But not for me the autumns as of yore,

But not for me the autumns as of yore.

floor, then returning to her former position, stands at the Shite *Seat.*

3

HERMIT   While absorbed in reciting the sutra, half-dreaming half-awake, I see a woman standing in the moonlight.   Who is out there?   *Rises.*

WOMAN   I am an inhabitant of the neighbourhood. Out of gratitude for the sutra most hard to meet with in any life,[1] I have come here to offer flowers and make obeisance so that I may enter upon Buddha's Way.

  Since you have found me out,

  May I make bold to ask your leave

  To enter for a while your cell

  And let my soul drink in the truth?

HERMIT   Indeed, it is meet and proper to partake of Truth, but as you are a woman and of such rare beauty,

  How can I let you in my cell?

WOMAN   I well understand your reason, but I am in some way bound to you:

  My home, too, is on Shōsui's banks,

HERMIT   Both draw water from it;

  Without our knowing it,

  A bond in a past life joined us;

WOMAN   I beg you, forbid me not your cell,

---

[1] Set phrase in praise of every Buddhist sutra. The verses to be recited before reading a sutra (關啓偈) aloud read: " This is the most high, most deep and most excellent Law, which is hard to meet in a hundred, a thousand, nay, ten thousand *kalpas*. Now that I am enabled to see, hear, and cherish it, may I also understand Buddha's real meaning."

HERMIT	" The shelter of the selfsame tree ! "[1]
CHORUS	Piercing the crumbling eaves and walls,
age-uta	The moon, too, lies on the dew-drenched floor,
	The moon, too, lies on the dew-drenched floor.

" Grim are the hills through which my pathway wends,

The WOMAN *dances while the following lines are chanted.*

Filling my soul with awe,

But when I see an ancient temple by the cliff,

Awesome sorrow melts away."[2]

How desolate is this moon-lit scene !

What poet wrote :

" Behind the screens of damask and brocade

You watch the flowers in the Palace garden ?"

But what comes next pleases me more :

" Within the hermit's cell I hear

The night rain falling on Mt. Rosan."[3]

The WOMAN *stops at the* Shite *Seat and turns to the* HERMIT.

4

HERMIT	As your zeal is so great, you may enter and listen while I recite the sutra.
WOMAN	Then I shall enter. How grateful I am ! As

Comes to the centre of the stage and sits down, facing the HER-MIT. *The latter sits*

---

[1] See *Tamura*, p. 32, note 1.

[2] Quotation from a sixteen-line poem by Tu Fu's (杜甫 ; eighth century Chinese poet) entitled "The Temple of Fa-ching (法鏡寺)," which begins with :

My personal safety being threatened,
I am seeking refuge in another province ;
I try to minimize the trouble,
But after all journey means pain,

followed by the lines quoted.

[3] In the original the four lines form a couplet by Po Chu-i (白居易 ; eighth century Chinese poet) quoted in the *Wakan Rōeishū*. Mt. Rosan is the Japanese for Mt. Lu-shan.

133

I listen, the words of the sutra bring hope not only to a woman such as I but also to insentient things like herbs and trees.

facing the Front audience and unrolling the sutra scroll, holds it up before him with both hands.

HERMIT You are indeed an intelligent listener. The great thing is to have a single mind filled with faith and gratitude, for then there is no room to doubt that even trees and herbs—nay all insentient things will attain salvation.

Turns towards her still holding the scroll.

WOMAN Indeed, a most blessed truth! Now, concerning the reason why trees and herbs can be saved,

Sir, I pray you, tell me more.

HERMIT The Parable of Medicinal Plants
Teaches us that all created things,
Be they possessed or not of sense,
Are all Reality.

Turning again towards the Front audience, the HERMIT looks at the sutra.
Turns towards the WOMAN.

WOMAN The gale on the peak,
HERMIT The stream in the vale,
WOMAN and HERMIT
Preach Buddha's Way.
Our hearts have grown now crystal-clear
As waters in the temple well.

CHORUS " Setting the lamp behind us, we gaze up
age-uta   at the moon,
Setting the lamp behind us, we gaze up at
the moon,
To enjoy the beauty of advancing night."[1]
With obedient heart
From the master's lips

The HERMIT rolls up the sutra and slips it back into his kimono.

---

[1] First half of a couplet by Po Chu-i contained in the *Wakan Rōeishū*. The second half reads:
Treading the fallen flowers,
We lament the passing spring of our youth.

I learn the inmost meaning of the holy
    words.
A faith that naught can shake
Shows me how to escape from the ' Burning
    House '[1]
That, fondly, we are so loth to quit.
That " green are the willows and pink the
    blossoms,"[2]
To the unclouded eye reveals
That plants of varied hues and scents
Are part of Buddha's shining land,
Are part of Buddha's shining land.

5

CHORUS	Is it not wonderful
rongi	A seemingly untutored woman
	Should have wit enough
	To unravel the doctrine's knotty points
	As clever fingers do a tangled skein?
WOMAN	Its truth is clear beyond all doubt.
	Did I not see the light to guide me
	Here and in the future's gloomy ways,
	I should not deem myself
	Worthy of the Way most hard to meet.
CHORUS	Happy it is to find the Way
	So hard to meet,
	To be born in the human world—

---

[1] In the ' Parable of the Burning House ' (see *Tōboku*, p. 85, note 3) it is written : " These three worlds are all unsafe, like a burning house ; they are filled with a multitude of dreadful pains."

[2] Common Zen Buddhist saying that expresses the identity of the phenomenal and the real. As Su Tung-po (蘇東坡 ; eleventh century Chinese poet) puts it :
The willows are green and the peach-blossoms are pink ;
They appear in their real aspect.

A fortune rare indeed ! [1]

WOMAN
CHORUS

That you should think me human
Makes me feel ashamed.
The full-orbed moon is shining bright
Upon my homeward path ;
The garden is white as driven snow.
If you should pierce this vain form of mine
Unreal as *bashō* leaves in snow,[2]
How could I hide my shame?
While thus she voices her uneasy thoughts,
A distant temple bell tolls,
" All is ephemeral,"[3]
" All is ephemeral,"
And she fades away.

The WOMAN *rises and looks towards the* Metsuke *Pillar. During the following lines she starts moving slowly towards the* Shite *Seat.*

The WOMAN *goes out.*

INTERLUDE

The MAN OF THE PLACE *enters the stage, wearing a striped kimono, sleeveless robe and trailing divided skirt, and short sword. Standing at the* Shite *Seat he tells the* HERMIT *that he has come to hear him read the sutra. Coming to the centre of the stage he sits down and enters into conversation with the hermit who questions him about the words "* bashō *leaves in snow."* *The* MAN *then tells the anecdote about a poet-painter who depicted a* bashō-*tree in the snow and explains that its leaves symbolize unreality.*

[1] It is a common Buddhist saying that the state of human beings is extremely difficult to acquire because it is the result of innumerable good deeds in past existences, and is even better than the lot of heavenly beings ; for while the latter are free from all pain and so lead too easy a life, the former are subject to frequent sufferings and sorrows which awaken in the mind the desire for salvation.

[2] Allusion to an anecdote about Wang Wei (王維 ; eighth century Chinese poet and painter) who is said to have painted a green *bashō*-tree covered with snow, an impossibility since its leaves wither in winter. Here it is used as a metaphor for the illusory nature of the heroine's female form.

[3] Buddhist temple bells are tolled at daybreak and sunset to warn the world of the transitoriness of all things.

PART TWO

1

HERMIT   The woman said her form was deceptive—
unreal as *bashō* leaves in snow. Now I know
for sure that the spirit of a *bashō*-tree—marvellous to tell—appeared to me in the likeness
of a woman.

machi-utai   The sutra worked that wonder,
The sutra worked that wonder!
Pondering upon this marvel
Fervently I read the sutra through the
    night;
Brighter and brighter grows the moon,
While the *bashō* leaves waft abroad
The Sacred Words.

2

While the entrance music issei *is being played, the*
SPIRIT OF THE BASHŌ-TREE *appears and advances
on to the stage, taking up her position at the* Shite
Seat. *She wears a* Fukai *mask, wig, painted gold-
patterned under-kimono, dancing* chōken *robe and
scarlet broad divided skirt.*

SPIRIT   See how the garden gleams in the pure light,
See how the garden gleams in the pure light!
Grateful am I, for, though the Blessed Law
Is rare as *udambara*[1] flowers,
Yet the Sacred Words
Fell like blessed rain on the *bashō*-tree.
See me now clothed in mortal shape,

Turns towards the
HERMIT.

[1] See *Sanemori*, p. 45, note 2.

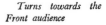

issei   Yet in this disguise
       I am indeed a flowerless plant—

CHORUS   An old *bashō*-tree such as you may find

SPIRIT   In any garden, field or hillside nook.

3

HERMIT   Watching and waiting all the night
       At last a form appears
       In likeness of my evening guest.
       Come, woman ! Who are you?

SPIRIT   I am not worthy of the name of woman.
   In truth I am an insentient being,
       A *bashō*-tree changed into woman.

HERMIT   A *bashō*-tree changed into woman?
       But through what cause
       Are you now clad in female form?

SPIRIT   You have no cause to marvel. No dividing
   line separates being from being.

HERMIT   Earth, herbs and trees

SPIRIT   Receive from heaven the selfsame dew and
       rain ;

HERMIT   Though unawares,
       Beings that cannot feel,

SPIRIT   Through them do grow and flourish.

HERMIT   Transformed because of this

SPIRIT   Into a foolish woman—

CHORUS   A frail thing, at best,—

age-uta   While still remaining a *bashō*-tree.
       The robe I wear is not pale blue[1]
       Which soon does fade;
       Its sleeves are sadly torn.

---

[1] In ancient Japan light-blue dye was obtained from the flowers of the *tsuyukusa* grass (*Commelina communis*), which was therefore called the 'flower-dye.' It faded very quickly.

What a disgrace!

4

CHORUS
kuri

Even non-sentient trees and herbs
Share Absolute Reality.
To the human mind
—A grain of dust, itself a universe [1]—
As water takes the form
Of rain or dew, or frost or snow,
So Reality does clothe itself
In countless forms.

The SPIRIT *stands in front of the Orchestra.*

SPIRIT
sashi
CHORUS

A spray of flowers offered to Buddha
Declares the Law that sways the world.
Lo! " A single bud unfolds
And spring has come for all."[2]
Under the warm rays of the spring sun
Willow and plum, damson and peach,

SPIRIT

All blossom, and their varied hues and
scents
Ravish men's hearts,

CHORUS

And yet all these are one, not separate,
Since every being shares the same reality.

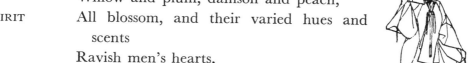

kuse

" The lofty palace by the water's edge
First catches the rising moon;
The budding trees that face the south
First greet the advancing spring."[3]
The works of Nature and its laws,
Displayed before the eye, delight the soul.
The spring goes by, the summer's passed;

The SPIRIT *dances while the following lines are chanted.*

---

[1] The *obiter dicta* of Yuan-wu (圜悟; twelfth century Chinese Zen abbot) contains the saying: " A grain of dust contains the universe; a split second grasps the whole world."

[2] In the *Ōjō Kōshiki* (Ritual for Invoking Rebirth in the Pure Land) it is written: " If a single bud unfolds, spring comes for all; if the mind once aspires to the Way, the whole world becomes the Way."

[3] Quotation from Su Lin (蘇鱗; Chinese poet of the Sung dynasty).

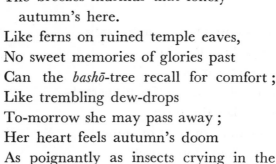

Stirring the garden reeds,
The breezes murmur that lonely
    autumn's here.
Like ferns on ruined temple eaves,
No sweet memories of glories past
Can the *basho*-tree recall for comfort;
Like trembling dew-drops
To-morrow she may pass away;
Her heart feels autumn's doom
As poignantly as insects crying in the
    grass.

SPIRIT   The elusiveness of life
         Brings to my mind the dream
CHORUS   Of the stag and the *basho* leaf;[1]
         In vain does the stag's cry pierce men's
             dreams.

The Western Mountain calls our souls,
Yet only few follow the westering moon.
Like bamboo-grasses tossed by autumn
    winds,
My mind is troubled
And I will rise and dance.

5

SPIRIT   To-night,
         Under the silvery moon
CHORUS   Ice my robe,
         Frost my skirt,

The SPIRIT *performs a* jo-no-mai *dance.*

---

[1] Allusion to a tale in *Lieh-tse* (列子) written by a Chinese philosopher of the same name, telling how once a wood-cutter on a hill saw a stag running past and killed it. Fearing some one might steal it, he hid it in a ditch under a *basho* leaf. But he soon forgot the place and when, after fruitless attempts, he was unable to find it again, came to the conclusion it must have only been a dream.

Warp of frost,
And woof of dew,
Gossamer-frail my robe.[1]

6

CHORUS	My sleeves of frail *bashō* leaves	*Dances while the following lines are chanted.*
SPIRIT	Are firm and deathless like the wings,	
CHORUS	Are firm and deathless like the wings	
	Of the blest heavenly maidens.[2]	
SPIRIT	Like them I wave my leafy sleeves	
CHORUS	Fanned by the rising winds	

Which blow across the temple courts
O'ergrown with *karukaya*[3] and *omina-eshi*.[4]
The wind becomes a gale,
And racing downwards bends the pines,
And tears up flowers and grasses,
And tears up flowers and grasses.
Alone stands the *bashō*,
Its leaves all torn to shreds.

The SPIRIT *stamps twice at the* Shite *Seat.*

[1] Quotation from Fujiwara-no-Sekio's poem in the *Kokinshū* which reads as follows:
> The brocade robe of the autumn hill,
> Being of warp of frost and woof of dew
> Hardly is it woven than it goes to pieces
> Because the material is so frail.

[2] From the transcendental point of view, no distinction is to be made between the two.

[3] I. e. *Themeda triandra*, a sedge-like grass common in open fields.

[4] I. e. *Patrinia scabiosaefolia*, an autumn plant with clusters of tiny yellow flowers.

SUMIDAGAWA

(The Sumida River)

.

CHORUS   How far I have come from home!
—Scene 3.

INTRODUCTION

Sumidagawa belongs to that division of the Fourth Group plays known as *kyōjo-mono* or ' mad woman ' piece. When they are bereaved mothers, the heroines in this division are represented as abnormally sensitive and peculiarly susceptible to their surroundings, and fall into fits of poetic exaltation which expresses itself by frenzied gestures. When their lost ones are found, their temporary madness leaves them. In this particular piece, however, the heroine discovers her lost child to be dead and the play ends on a tragic note, not usual in ' mad woman ' pieces.

The scene is laid on both banks of the river Sumida and on the river itself. The place where the incident is supposed to have occurred is situated on the river near the present Asakusa in Tokyo which was then open country. As the Sumida ferryman is about to row across, a traveller appears, who asks to be ferried over, and is followed shortly after by a distraught mother who, for many months, has been seeking her only child. It is a spring evening. At the sight of white birds floating here and there on the river, the mad woman recalls a poem in the *Ise Monogatari*, which awakens in her a frenzied longing for her child, which finds dramatic expression in a *kakeri* dance.

The scene that follows takes place on the ferry. Questioned as to the meaning of the solemn chanting across the river, the ferryman tells the traveller that on that very day a year before a kidnapped boy was struck down by sudden illness, and was left by the slaver to die on the roadside. The kind-hearted villagers who subsequently buried him on the bank of the river are now holding a memorial service for the repose of his soul. Hearing the sad story, the mad woman guesses that the child is indeed her long-sought boy and that she has reached the end of her quest. In the concluding scene the grieving mother is led to a grassy mound by a willow-tree under which the child was buried, and is asked by the villagers to lead their prayers to Amida Buddha. While they are chanting, the child repeatedly appears before her eyes, only to fade away every time she attempts to clasp him in her arms. Finally as dawn breaks, the ghost vanishes for ever into the mound, leaving her disconsolate.

145

Author: Jūrō Motomasa (1395–1459), son of Zeami Motokiyo.
Source: None has as yet been ascertained. It seems likely that the author based his plot on some ancient legend or contemporary incident.

SUMIDAGAWA

Persons

FERRYMAN OF THE SUMIDA RIVER	*Waki*
TRAVELLER FROM MIYAKO	*Waki-zure*
MOTHER, A MAD WOMAN	*Shite*
GHOST OF UMEWAKA-MARU, HER CHILD	*Kokata*

Place

Sumida River, Musashi Province

Season

Spring

Stage-attendants place a framework mound covered with willow branches in front of the Orchestra, inside which the ghost-child is hidden.

1

While the entrance music nanoribue *is being played, the* FERRYMAN OF THE SUMIDA RIVER *enters the stage and stands at the* Shite *Seat. He wears a striped kimono,* suō *robe and trailing divided skirt.*

FERRYMAN I am he who rows the ferry across the Sumida in the province of Musashi. To-day I must quickly ferry people across the water because we are holding a solemn memorial service[1]

---

[1] The tomb of Umewaka is in the precincts of the Mokubo-ji, a small temple on the left bank of the river Sumida, roughly opposite the present Asakusa. Since the temple is believed to have been built after the present play became popular, it is very doubtful the tomb is really that of Umewaka.

for someone at the village on the other side of the river where both priest and laymen are gathering in great numbers. Mark this well, all of you !

Sits down in front of the CHORUS.

2

While the entrance music shidai *is being played, the* TRAVELLER FROM MIYAKO *enters with a mushroom hat on. He wears a striped kimono,* kakesuō *robe and white broad divided skirt.*

TRAVELLER shidai	To the far Eastland I am bound, To the far Eastland I am bound ; Tedious days of travel lie before me.
CHORUS jidori	To the far Eastland I am bound ; Tedious days of travel lie before me.

TRAVELLER I come from Miyako. I have a friend in the Eastland and now I am going there to visit him.

Removes his hat.

michi-yuki   Behind me wrapt in clouds and mists
Lie the mountains I have crossed,
Lie the mountains I have crossed.
Many a barrier have I passed through,
Many a province have I traversed.
Here lies the far-famed Sumida,
And now I have reached the ferry,
And now I have reached the ferry.

Puts it on again.

Travelling in haste, here I am
at the Sumida ferry and over there
I see a ferry-boat about to leave.
I will make haste and board it.
Hi boatman ! I want to get in
your boat.

Removes his hat.

FERRYMAN All right sir ! Get in. But first may I ask *Rises* you what is the meaning of that unusual noise from where you have just come?

TRAVELLER It is a crazy woman from Miyako and people are amused by her mad dancing.

FERRYMAN Then I will delay the ferry-boat for a while *Sits on the* Waki and wait for the mad creature. *Seat to the right of the* TRAVELLER.

3

While the entrance music issei *is being played, the* MOTHER *appears and stops on the Bridgeway by the First Pine. She wears a* Fukai *mask, wig, painted gold-patterned under-kimono, embroidered* koshimaki *outer-kimono, broad-sleeved robe. She has on a mushroom hat, and carries a spray of bamboo.*

MOTHER   " Although a mother's mind
sashi   May be unclouded,
               She well may lose her way
               Through love of her child."[1]
               How true that is !
               Where does my darling stray?
               Shall I ask these travellers?
               Does he know his mother's grief?
               " Does not the skyey wind
CHORUS   Whisper to the waiting pines? "[2]

---

[1] Poem by Fujiwara-no-Kanesuke contained in the *Gosenshū*.
[2] Poem by Lady Kunaikyō included in the *Shin Kokinshū*. In its complete form it reads :
        Has he (the lover) not heard the saying,
        That even the wind blowing
        Through the upper regions of the sky
        Does not disdain to visit the pine?
The word ' pine ' has a double meaning of ' tree ' and ' pining heart.'

The MOTHER *advances on to the stage and per-*
forms a kakeri *dance.*

MOTHER   In this world fleeting like the dews
              Upon Makuzu Field,[1]

CHORUS   Should I thus pass my days
              Complaining of my bitter day?

MOTHER   For many years I lived
sashi   In Miyako, at Kita-Shirakawa[2];

              Then suddenly I lost my only child,
              Kidnapped by a slaver.
              They told me he was taken
              Beyond the Ōsaka Barrier[3]
              Eastwards, to far-off Azuma,[4]
              Since when with mind distraught
              I wander on my desperate quest,
              Torn by longing for my boy.   *Weeps.*

CHORUS   " Though he be a thousand miles away
sage-uta —'Tis said—a mother ne'er forgets her child,"[5]
age-uta   And yet the bond of parenthood
              Cannot survive the grave,
              Cannot survive the grave.[6]
              Ah! Woe is me

              That even in this world I must be parted
                 from him
              Like the " four young birds that left their
                 nest."[7]

[1] Field at the foot of Higashiyama Hill in Kyoto, where there is now Maruyama Park.

[2] Eastern suburbs of Miyako.

[3] See *Tamura*, p. 34, note 1.

[4] I.e. Eastland. See *Tamura*, p. 23, note 1.

[5] Quoted from a poem by Po Chu-i which more exactly reads : " A parent may go a thousand miles from home, but he never can forget his child."

[6] Due probably to a Buddhist theory it was currently believed that the bond between parent and child lasts only during the present life while that between man and wife endures for two lives.

[7] Allusion to a conversation between Confucius and Yen Hui (顏回) found in the *Words and Deeds of Confucius* (孔子家語) where it is told that once, very early in the morning, Confucius was sitting with his disciple Yen Hui. Hearing very mournful cries, the master enquired what they were, whereupon the

Will my weary quest end here?
Now I have reached the Sumida,
Now I have reached the Sumida
That flows between Musashi and Shimōsa.

MOTHER　Pray, boatman. Let me get into the boat.

FERRYMAN　Where are you from and where are you going?

MOTHER　From Miyako I have come in search of someone.

FERRYMAN　Since you are a woman of Miyako and mad to boot, I will not take you aboard unless you amuse us with one of your crazy dances.

MOTHER　What a clumsy way of speaking! Since you are the Sumida ferryman, you should have answered, "Come on board, for the day is spent,"[1]

Yet you refuse a passage
To me, a city lady.
How ill-becoming a Su-
mida boatman
To speak so rudely!

FERRYMAN　How like a woman of Miyako to use such elegant language!

MOTHER　Your words remind me of the poem Narihira once composed at this very spot.

" O, birds of Miyako,
If you are worthy of your name,

pupil replied that they could not be lamentations over the dead, and told him the story of a bird which had built its nest on Mt. Han-shan. When the four young birds it had reared had grown up and prepared to leave the nest, the mother-bird had uttered heart-rending cries not unlike those they were now hearing. Upon enquiring from the neighbour it turned out that the master had died and that in order to defray his funeral expenses, the family had been obliged to sell one of the children into slavery, and were now about to part from him for ever. Confucius praises his pupil for his keenness in distinguishing voices.

[1] Quoted from the *Ise Monogatari*, chap. viii, where Narihira, the supposed author, describes his travels through the Eastland in search of a place to settle in, after his life in Miyako had become too unpleasant. The chapter ends with his crossing the river Sumida.

Tell me, does my love still live? "[1]

O, boatman, yonder is a white bird not found *Turns towards the right.*
in Miyako.   What is its name?

FERRYMAN   It is a sea-gull.

MOTHER   How unpoetical! By the sea you may call
it a gull or a plover or whatever you will, but
here by the Sumida river why not " Miyako-
bird? "

FERRYMAN   Truly I was in the wrong!
Living in this famous place
'Twas thoughtless of me,
Instead of Miyako-bird,

MOTHER   To call it sea-gull.

FERRYMAN   So Narihira long ago

MOTHER   Asked, " Is she still alive? "

FERRYMAN   Remembering his lady in Miyako.

MOTHER   Moved by like yearning,
I am seeking my lost child
In the Eastland.

FERRYMAN   To long for a sweetheart,

MOTHER   To seek after a lost child,

FERRYMAN   Both spring

MOTHER   From love.

CHORUS   O, Miyako-bird, I too will ask you,

age-uta   O, Miyako-bird, I too will ask you,
Is my dear child still living
Somewhere in the Eastland?
I ask and ask, but it will not answer.
Oh, rude Miyako-bird!
I'll call you ' rustic-bird.'
" By the River Horie

*The MOTHER turns
towards the Waki
Front.*

---

[1] Quoted from the same. ' Miyako-bird ' is a poetic name for sea-gull.

Where boats hurry past each other,
Miyako-birds utter their cries : "[1]
There at Naniwa in the West,
Here by the Sumida in the East—
How far I have come from home !
But, pray, O boatman,
Let me come on board.
Though crowded be your boat,
O, let me too on board, I pray !

She goes to the First Pine and touching the brim of her hat gazes into the distance.

Returning from the Bridgeway, she goes up to the FERRYMAN *and dropping the spray of bamboo, joins her hands in supplication.*

FERRYMAN   So sensible a mad woman I never saw. Be
quick and come aboard. This is a dangerous
crossing ; please take care and sit still. You
too, traveller, get in.

Slips his right arm out of his kimono and picks up his pole.
The MOTHER *removes her hat and holding it in her left hand, steps forward as if getting into a boat and sits down. The* TRAVELLER *sits sideways behind the* MOTHER *while the* FERRYMAN *stands at the back and plies his pole.*

4

TRAVELLER   Why are all those people gathered together
over there, under that willow-tree?

FERRYMAN   They are holding a solemn memorial service
connected with a sad tale which I shall tell you
while the boat is crossing to the other side.

katari   It happened last year, on the fifteenth of the
third month ; yes, and this is the very day on
which it happened. A slave-trader was on his
way to the Northeast, taking along with him
a boy he had bought—a tender lad some
twelve years old. Wearied out by the un-
accustomed hardships of the road, the boy
was seized with a mortal illness. He was so
weak, he said he could not drag himself a
step farther, and lay down on the bank.
What heartless men there are in this world !

---

[1] Poem by Ōtomo-no-Yakamochi contained in the *Manyōshū*.

The slaver abandoned the boy by the roadside and went on his way.

But the people of this neighbourhood, judging from his appearance that the lad was of gentle birth, nursed and tended him as best they could. But perhaps because of his *karma*, he grew worse and worse. When he was at the point of death, we asked him, " Where were you born, who are you? " " I was born in Miyako—he replied—at Kita-Shirakawa, the only child of Lord Yoshida. My father being dead, mother and I lived alone. Then I was kidnapped and now am brought to this pass. Please bury me here by the roadside, so that passers-by coming from dear Miyako may at least cast their shadow over my grave: and plant a willow-tree in memory of me." He said these words, calmly, like a man ; invoked Amida Buddha several times, and died. What a piteous happening !

The MOTHER *weeps.*

There may be some people from Miyako in this boat. Let them offer prayers for the repose of his poor soul, even if they are not relations of the dead lad. Look! While you were listening to my long and tedious tale, the ferry has reached the bank. Make haste and land !

TRAVELLER I will surely remain here to-day and though I had nothing to do with the lad, I will offer up a prayer for him.

Going to the Waki Seat, addresses the FERRYMAN *and then sits down.*

FERRYMAN Come, my mad creature there ! Why not get out of my boat? Hurry ! How tender-

Turns and looks at the weeping MOTHER.

154

hearted of you to shed tears over such a story. Please get out of the boat quickly!

MOTHER   Boatman, when did the event you have just told us take place? *Turns to the FERRYMAN.*

FERRYMAN It took place last year, in the third month, on this very day.

MOTHER   What was the lad's age?

FERRYMAN Twelve.

MOTHER   His name?

FERRYMAN Umewaka-maru.

MOTHER   And his father's name?

FERRYMAN Lord Yoshida.

MOTHER   Since then have neither of his parents been here?

FERRYMAN Nor any of his kin.

MOTHER   Much less his mother!

FERRYMAN No, that would have been out of the question.

MOTHER   No wonder, neither kin nor parent came.
He was the child
This mad woman is seeking.
Is this a dream?
O cruel fate! *Lets fall her hat and weeps.*

FERRYMAN Who on earth could have dreamt of such a thing? Until now I thought it was none of our business. The boy was your child. You are to be pitied! Now let me show you where the boy is buried. Please come with me. *Puts away his pole and standing behind her, helps her out of the boat, then takes a few steps towards the mound.*

5

FERRYMAN This is the grave of your dead child. Pray for his soul's repose, as only you can do. *Goes to the Waki Seat and sits down.*

155

MOTHER	I had hoped against hope
	To find my child
	And now I have reached strange Azuma,
	He is no more upon this earth ;
	Naught but this mound remains.
	O, how cruel !
	Was it for this that he was born,
	To be taken from his native land,
	To the remotest part of Azuma,
	Only to become dust by the roadside ?
	Does my dear child truly lie beneath this grass ?

Moves to the left, half facing the mound and sits gazing at it.

Half rises and fixes her eyes on the mound.

CHORUS	O you people there,
sage-uta	Dig up the sod
	So that I may once again
	Gaze on his mortal form.

The MOTHER turns towards the FERRY-MAN and moves her hana as if to dig, then subsides on to the stage and weeps.

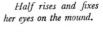

age-uta	He whose life was full of promise is gone,
	He whose life was full of promise is gone,
	And she whose life is worthless left behind.
	Before the mother's eyes the son appears
	And fades away
	As does the phantom broom-tree.[1]
	In this grief-laden world
	Such is the course of human life.
	The winds of death

---

[1] Mythical tree shaped like a broom said to have stood in a village called Sonohara on the boundary between Shinano and Mino Provinces. It had the mysterious property of being seen clearly from afar, but of disappearing when anyone approached closer.

Scatter the spring-time flowers of life;
The clouds of mutability
O'ercast the shining moon
That should light up the endless night of
    life and death.[1]
Now my eyes see how fleeting is this life,
Now my eyes see how fleeting is this life.

6

FERRYMAN Your tears no longer serve; chant but your
prayers for his repose in the other world.
    The moon has risen,
    The river breeze is blowing,
    The night is at its height,
    'Tis time we began our night prayers.
    Asking her to join them
    They start to beat their gongs.

Stands up, holding a disc-like gong and a wooden hammer.

Striking his gong, turns towards the MOTHER.

MOTHER   O'erwhelmed by grief
    The mother cannot say her prayer,
    But prostrate weeps upon the ground.

FERRYMAN This is not as it should be. However many
people may gather together, it is a mother's
prayers that will rejoice her dead child.
    So saying he hands the gong to the
    mother.

After giving her the gong and hammer, he takes his place in front of the CHORUS.

MOTHER   You say true—
    I'll take the gong
    For my child's sake.

Rises and faces the mound.

FERRYMAN Ceasing her moan, in a clear voice
MOTHER   She prays with them under the shining
    moon.

[1] The full moon is likened to Sakyamuni who dispels the darkness of ignorance and enlightens mortal minds.

FERRYMAN   Her thoughts wing straight
To the Western Land of
Bliss.

FERRYMAN and MOTHER
Adoration to countless
million Buddhas—
Each one Amida
In the Western Paradise,[1]
The world of supreme bliss !

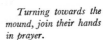

Turning towards the mound, join their hands in prayer.

CHORUS   Namu Amida ! Namu Amida !
Namu Amida ! Namu Amida !

MOTHER   From the Sumida
Join in the voices
Of the breeze and waves.

The MOTHER beats the gong, accompanying the invocation.

CHORUS   Namu Amida ! Namu Amida !
Namu Amida !

MOTHER   True to their name
Miyako-birds join the choir.

GHOST and CHORUS
Namu Amida ! Namu Amida !
Namu Amida !

Faces the Front audience.
The voice of the GHOST of Umewaka-maru is heard from inside the mound.

MOTHER   Surely just now among them I heard my
child's voice. He seems to be praying inside
this mound.

Ceases to beat her gong.

FERRYMAN We, too, have heard your child. We shall
keep silent ; say your prayer alone.

---

¹ *Lung-shu Jōdomon* (龍舒淨土文; Collection of Texts relating to the Western Paradise, edited in Lung-shu by a man of the Southern Sung dynasty) states that seeing an aged couple assiduously repeating the *nembutsu* prayer and using a bagful of seeds to mark the number of repetitions, Sakyamuni was filled with pity at their pious device, and taught them a better means of doing so by saying : " Namu to the thirty-six trillion, one hundred and nineteen thousand five hundred Amida Buddhas of the Western Paradise, all having the same name and title."

MOTHER   O that I might hear his voice but once again !

Namu Amida !

GHOST   Namu Amida ! Namo Amida !

CHORUS   See, his voice and shape !

Turns towards the mound and strikes the gong.

The GHOST OF UMEWAKA-MARU comes out of the mound and stands in front of the Waki Seat. He wears a flowing black-hair wig, white broad-sleeved robe and white twill kimono.

MOTHER   Is it you, my child?

GHOST   Is it you, my mother?

CHORUS   And as she seeks to grasp it by the hand,

The shape begins to fade away ;

The vision fades and reappears

And stronger grows her yearning.

Day breaks in the eastern sky.

The ghost has vanished ;

What seemed her boy

Is but a grassy mound

Lost on the wide, desolate moor.

Sadness and tender pity fill all hearts,

Sadness and tender pity fill all hearts !

Turns towards the MOTHER.

The MOTHER drops the gong and hammer and runs up to the GHOST, who retreats and re-enters the mound. Dazed and weeping, she looks up and moves two or three steps towards the Shite Pillar. The GHOST reappears and stands at the Shite Seat. With stretched arms the MOTHER runs towards it, and attempts to embrace it, but as the GHOST retreats again into the mound, the MOTHER falls, clasping the empty air. Rising again she approaches the mound, gazing at the willow-branches, then, disconsolate, retreats slowly to the Shite Pillar and remains there weeping.

159

FUNA-BENKEI

(Benkei in the Boat)

TOMOMORI   I, Tomomori,
CHORUS   Will drag down Yoshitsune
            Under the waves beneath which I sank.
                      —Part II, scene 5.

INTRODUCTION

Funa-Benkei is a *hataraki-mono* or 'war-dance' piece of the *Kiri* Noh group. Its peculiarity is that the *waki*, contrary to the general practice, is assigned a role no less important than that of the *shite*, although the *shite* still remains the protagonist, thus adding to the dramatic effect.

On account of his resounding victories, the Hōgan[1] Yoshitsune[2] came to be suspected of disloyalty by his brother the Shogun Yoritomo[3] and thought it

---

[1] Title given to a secondary officer in the police and judicial office charged with maintaining peace and order in Miyako.

[2, 3] Yoritomo and Yoshitsune were half-brothers, sons of Yoshitomo, chief of the Minamoto family, but by different mothers, a circumstance noteworthy because in those days the relative importance of brothers in a noble family depended upon the social position of their mothers' families. As Yoshitsune's mother came from a family of no importance, Yoritomo, apart from private feelings, was justified in treating his half-brother hardly better than a retainer. When they were very young, the two great families of Minamoto (Genji) and Taira (Heike) were almost equally matched rivals from the military point of view, each having numerous followers in the provinces. In the unsuccessful *coup d'état* of Heiji (1159), however, the Genji which supported the rebels were utterly crushed by the Heike, and the head of the family was killed, while Yoritomo, then a boy of twelve, was banished to a remote province, and Yoshitsune finally managed to take refuge with a powerful independent family in the extreme north of Japan. After some thirty years, when Yoritomo started a war against the Heike, Yoshitsune joined him and was appointed commander of an army. His first exploit was to defeat and destroy Minamoto-no-Yoshinaka (see *Sanemori*, p. 39, note 1) who, having started on a separate campaign, anticipated Yoritomo's armies in entry into Miyako and made the Imperial court confer on him the title of Shogun.

The Heike routed from the capital, fled to the provinces bordering on the Inland Sea, taking with them the infant emperor. It was chiefly due to Yoshitsune's brilliant generalship that after fifteen months during which he inflicted two signal defeats on them at Ichinotani near Kobe, and at Yashima near Takamatsu in Shikoku, the Heike were totally annihilated in the Straits of Bakan. Despite these exploits discord was destined to break out between the brothers. Determined to quell the proud and insubordinate to his own authority, Yoritomo forbade his followers to receive any appointments or honours from the Emperor except at his recommendation. Yoshitsune, however, presuming upon his blood-relationship, allowed himself to be appointed Hōgan without Yoritomo's permission.

This breach of discipline highly angered the Shogun and when Yoshitsune took the most important Heike captives—including the head of the family and his heir—down to Kamakura, then the seat of the Shogunate, he was forbidden to enter that town, much less to see his elder brother. His repeated apologies and petitions having failed to appease Yoritomo, Yoshitsune in turn naturally became angry, and threatened to become the leader of those, whether at court or among the military, who were discontent with the Kamakura government. Two attempts were made upon his life by envoys sent to Miyako by the Kamakura government on specious missions. Finding it unsafe to remain longer in Miyako, Yoshitsune, accompanied by a handful of personal retainers and his faithful mistress Shizuka, went down to Osaka in order to take boat from there to Kyūshū and thus place himself in safety.

prudent secretly to leave Miyako for the Westland,[1] and there in safety to await the event.

The play consists of two parts: the first deals with the Hōgan's parting from his mistress Shizuka[2] at Daimotsu Bay[3]; the second with a very dramatic sea-fight between Benkei, his faithful retainer and the ghost of the drowned Tomo-mori,[4] one of the Heike chiefs, who was attempting to sink their boat in revenge for his defeat.

[1] In its broad sense, the Westland refers to the provinces west of Miyako but in the present case it specifically means the island of Kyūshū.

[2] Dancer (late twelfth century) who was the daughter of Iso-no-Zenji of the same profession. The mother is said to have started the new style of solo dancing called *shira-byōshi* (white-robed singing and dancing) which soon became the fashion in Miyako. The cleverest artistes of this school were patronized by the nobility as in the case of the Giō and Gijo sisters and later of Hotoke who became ladies of Taira-no-Kiyomori's harem (*The Heike Monogatari*, Vol. I). While Hōgan in Miyako, Yoshitsune was captivated by Shizuka's beauty and art, and made her his mistress. When Tosabō Shōshun, an emissary from Kamakura, tried with a party of warriors to murder Yoshitsune in a treacherous night attack on his mansion, Shizuka's vigilance and courage were mainly responsible for saving her lord's life. Later she accompanied him on his unsuccessful journey to Kyūshū. The present play is based on the latter event and, although according to it she was prevented from embarking at Daimotsu Bay, she is mentioned in a fourteenth century version of the story (*Gikeiki*, i.e. History of Yoshitsune) as having been in one of the boats when a sudden storm frustrated Yoshitsune's plan of sailing to the Westland. Subsequently she was one of the small party of followers who sought sanctuary with him in the Yoshino Mountains. When the Hōgan decided to undertake a perilous journey to the north disguised as a 'mountain ascetic,' Shizuka was sent home to her mother accompanied by two or three servants who, however, robbed her of all valuable parting gifts given her by Yoshitsune and treacherously deserted her in the wilderness. She then fell into the hands of monks belonging to a Buddhist monastery who were eager to curry favour with the Kamakura government by capturing Yoshitsune. Finally, when sent down to Kamakura to be questioned as to the whereabouts of her lord, Shizuka firmly refused to give him away, and having been found with child by Yoshitsune, was detained at Kamakura till after her accouchement. Meanwhile Yoritomo's wife Masako, having heard of her fame as a dancer, wished her to perform before Yoritomo and his retinue at one of the Hachiman shrines. Though reluctantly, Shizuka consented to display her art to the great admiration of the audience, but at an encore she boldly expressed her longing for her lord by singing two ancient poems which voiced similar sentiments to the great displeasure of Yoritomo, but escaped punishment thanks to his wife's entreaties (the above incident is touched upon in a Noh play entitled *Futari Shizuka*, i.e. Double Shizuka). In due course she gave birth to a boy who was snatched from her and drowned in the sea of Kamakura. What happened to her subsequently has not been recorded.

[3] Bay situated to the southwest of Amagasaki, Settsu Province.

[4] Fourth son of Kiyomori. Pre-eminent in wisdom and valour, he was the right-hand man of Munemori, Kiyomori's unworthy successor. When Prince Mochihito was rallying the disaffected elements Tomomori quickly nipped the movement in the bud, slaying the prince and other leaders at the battle of Uji and destroying the Genji in the neighbouring province of Ōmi. When, alarmed by the rapid advance of Yoshinaka on Miyako, it was proposed to move the Imperial capital to Fukuhara near Kobe, Tomomori opposed this cowardly plan, insisting that they should defend the capital to the last. His counsel, however, did not prevail, and when the removal was carried out it was found that the Imperial party was reduced to the infant emperor, grandson of Kiyomori, and to the Imperial dowager, his

In Part One the *shite* is a beautiful lady who performs a *chū-no-mai* dance ; that in Part Two the ghost of a warrior who performs a *hataraki* dance. The *waki* is played throughout by Benkei who preserves his lord's honour by causing Shizuka to return to Miyako, and afterwards saves his life by invoking the deities of the five quarters.[1] The Hōgan, a secondary role, is played by the *kokata* for, according to the conventions of the Noh drama, only two leading parts are allowed. In the present play the role of the *kyōgen* has an unusually dramatic significance in that he is the chief boatman upon whose convincing acting full realization of the storm scene mainly depends.

Author : Kwanze Kojirō Nobumitsu (1435–1516)

Source : *Heike Monogatari* (Tale of the Heike) and *Gempei Seisuiki* (Rise and Fall of the Genji and the Heike) which give the details of the Hōgan's flight. The source from which the author has derived the latter's separation from Shizuka and his encounter with Tomomori's ghost has not yet been ascertained.

---

daughter and the Heike nobles. In 1184, less than two years later, the Heike were annihilated at the Straits of Bakan and, seeing that all was lost, Tomomori persuaded Kiyomori's widow to throw herself into the sea together with the emperor in order to avoid the disgrace of captivity. Munemori also plunged into the sea, but being a good swimmer he kept afloat and was captured. Angered at this shameful slight to the honour of a military family, Tomomori with his sword put an end to his own life.

[1] See p. 182, note 1.

165

FUNA-BENKEI

(BENKEI IN THE BOAT)

Persons

HŌGAN, MINAMOTO-NO-YOSHITSUNE	*Kokata*
MUSASHIBŌ BENKEI	*Waki*
THREE RETAINERS OF THE HŌGAN	*Waki-zure*
CHIEF BOATMAN	*Kyōgen*
LADY SHIZUKA	*Shite* in Part One
GHOST OF TAIRA-NO-TOMOMORI	*Shite* in Part Two

Place

Shore of Daimotsu Bay, Settsu Province (Part One)
Sea off Daimotsu Bay (Part Two)

Season

Autumn

PART ONE

1

While the entrance music shidai *is being played, the* HŌGAN *with his* THREE RETAINERS *and* BENKEI *appear and advance on to the stage. The* HŌGAN *wears a tall black cap, heavy silk kimono, soba-tsugi robe, white broad divided skirt and sword.* BENKEI *wears a small round cap, brocade stole, heavy silk kimono, broad-sleeved robe, white broad divided*

167

*skirt, short sword and carries a rosary of diamond-
shaped beads. The THREE RETAINERS wear costumes
similar to those of their lord and short swords.*

BENKEI and RETAINERS

shidai   To-day we start upon our journey,

      To-day we start upon our journey;

      But when shall we see Miyako again?

CHORUS   To-day we start upon our journey;

jidori   But when shall we see Miyako again?

BENKEI   I am Musashibō Benkei of the Western
Quarter.[1] My lord the Hōgan, as Yoritomo's
Lieutenant, has vanquished the Heike clan.
The relations between them
should be brotherly as those
of sun and moon, but to
our deep regret some despica-
ble mischief-maker[2] has sown
discord between them. Out of
regard for his brother, my lord is however leaving Miyako for a while and going down to the
Westland, to send from there a petition to his
brother proving his innocence. To-day before
dawn he hastens to Yodo[3] to take a boat for
Amagasaki on the Bay of Daimotsu in the province of Settsu.

---

[1] Mt. Hiei near Kyoto, headquarters of the Tendai sect of Buddhism since the ninth century, once numbered several hundred temples and monasteries. These were divided into three groups, of which the Western Quarter was one, the others being the Eastern Quarter and the Yokawa Quarter.

[2] Refers to Kajiwara-no-Kagetoki, an influential Genji captain under Yoshitsune when the latter commanded one of the Genji expeditionary armies against the Heike. During the council of war held on the eve of the battle of Yashima in Shikoku, a fierce quarrel broke out between them. Harbouring resentment against his general, on his return to Kamakura, Kagetoki slandered Yoshitsune to his elder brother the Shogun Yoritomo, thus causing the brothers to become estranged.

[3] See *Eguchi*, p. 114, note 1.

Benkei and Retainers
sashi   It is early in the era of Bunji ;
           Open discord has broken out
           Between Yoritomo and Yoshitsune.
           Uncertain what to do,
Hōgan   The Hōgan leaves Miyako,
           And ere all roads are closed to him,[1]
           Westwards he makes his way

Benkei and Retainers
           And quits Miyako before dawn.
           As the moon climbs the sky,
           His thoughts linger behind.
           Unlike when years ago [2] he started
             hence
           Against the rebel Heike troops,
           Now with heavy heart he mounts the boat
           With a small band of trusty followers.

sage-uta   Uncertain is the lot of man,
           As floating clouds and running water !
age-uta   " In this world—
           Say what people may,
           Say what people may,
           The God of Rock-spring knows
           The man whose heart is pure."[3]
           So towards his holy shrine from afar
           Reverently we bow our heads.
           And soon—where travellers' weary thoughts

---

[1] Yoritomo, jealous of his brother's fame, determined to get rid of him. Several attempts on his life having already been made, it was now feared, as later events were to prove, that Government orders would be issued to the lords responsible for guarding the barriers on the principal roads to examine strictly all travellers in order to intercept Yoshitsune and his followers.

[2] I.e. 1185 when Yoshitsune was preparing to attack the Heike at Yashima in the Inland Sea.

[3] Poem attributed to the God of the Iwashimizu (rock-spring) Temple in the southern suburbs of Kyoto.

> Are swept away by waves and ebbing tides—
> Daimotsu Bay is reached,
> Daimotsu Bay is reached.

BENKEI Travelling in haste, we have now reached the shore of Daimotsu Bay. As I have an acquaintance here, I will go and ask him to give us shelter.

FIRST RETAINER

That will be good.

2

BENKEI Excuse me. Is the master of the house at home?

BENKEI goes to the Shite Pillar and turns towards the Bridgeway.

The BOATMAN, *who is sitting at the* Kyōgen *Seat, rises and goes to the First Pine. He wears a check-patterned kimono,* kyōgen *robe and divided skirt.*

BOATMAN Who is asking for me?

BENKEI Musashi is my name.

BOATMAN What brings you here this time?

BENKEI I have come with my lord. Please give him lodging.

BOATMAN With pleasure.

BENKEI As he is travelling incognito, please prepare the inner room for him and make ready a boat as well, because he must leave for the Westland.

The HŌGAN *and others go to the* Waki *Seat. The* HŌGAN *sits on a stool while* BENKEI *and* RETAINERS *sit near him on the floor in front of the* CHORUS. *The* BOATMAN *retires to the Kyōgen Seat.*

BOATMAN Certainly. May it please your lordship, come into the inner room.

BENKEI May it please my lord, though I hesitate to mention it, I now see that Lady Shizuka is coming with us. Under the circumstances it seems unsuitable; it would be well if she were firmly ordered to return home.

Approaching the HŌGAN, *kneels down and bows deeply.*

170

HŌGAN   Let Benkei deal with this matter as he thinks best.

BENKEI   Very well, my lord. I will go to Lady Shizuka's lodgings and convey to her your lordship's decision.

3

BENKEI   Ho, you there! Is Lady Shizuka staying in this house? Musashi comes as messenger from his lord.

Goes to the First Pine and speaks towards the Curtain.

LADY SHIZUKA *enters and advances to the Third Pine. She wears a 'young woman' mask, wig, painted gold-patterned under-kimono and brocade outer-kimono.*

SHIZUKA   Musashi? Little had I expected him! What matter brought your reverence here?

BENKEI   The matter stands like this. My lord wishes you to know he greatly appreciates your coming all this way, but desires that you should return to Miyako, as your presence is no longer becoming under the circumstances.

SHIZUKA   I never should have expected this of him! I had determined to follow him wherever he might go.

However much you trust it,
The human heart proves fickle.
Alas! Your message has hurt me deeply.   *Weeps.*

BENKEI   What answer shall I take back to my lord?

SHIZUKA   If my coming with him should cause him any trouble, then I will stay behind.

BENKEI   You are taking the matter too seriously. But you should stay behind.

171

SHIZUKA   The more I think of it, the more I am con-
vinced that Musashi has made this up.—I will
come myself to the HŌGAN and give him my
answer.

BENKEI   Do so if you wish. I shall accompany you.

4

BENKEI   May it please my lord, Lady Shizuka is here.

HŌGAN   Listen to me, Shizuka. Though I have suddenly become a fugitive from Miyako, you have
followed me as far as here. I duly ap-
preciate your devotion. It would not
be well, however, for you to travel far
across the rough seas. Return to Miyako
for the time being and await me there.

*LADY SHIZUKA and
BENKEI advance to the
centre of the stage and
sit down.*

SHIZUKA   So that is truly my lord's will ! How wrong
it was of me to have felt reproachful towards
innocent Musashi !
Indeed I feel ashamed !

BENKEI   No, no, do not mind about me, my lady. My
lord only fears what people may say.
       Think not his love has failed ;
       Thus says Benkei shedding tears.

SHIZUKA   Nay, worthless creature that I am,
       Even though forsaken,
       I harbour no reproach ;
       But since you are about to sail the seas,

CHORUS   How can my lord leave Shizuka behind,
age-uta   How can my lord leave Shizuka behind,
       Since ' shizuka ' means calm weather?
       The enduring troth we plighted
       Calling the gods to witness
       Has been of no avail ;

"I hold my life more dear
Than parting from my lord,
For I would see my lord again
In days to come."[1]

SHIZUKA *weeps.*

5

HŌGAN — Here Benkei! Serve wine to Shizuka.

BENKEI — Certainly, my lord. This cup of chrysanthe-
mum wine, to speed him on his journey and wish
my lord may live for countless years,
Benkei now offers to Shizuka.

*With his fan, makes
the gesture of filling
her cup.*

SHIZUKA — Now I must leave my lord ;
O'erwhelmed by endless sorrow,
Tears choke me

BENKEI — And with good reason. But will you not
sing a song of farewell
And dance for him?

SHIZUKA — Shizuka arises
And sings the song of leave-taking ;
"The wind has dropped,
The ferry-boat leaves the haven ;

CHORUS — As the skies clear,
The land of exile looms across the waves."[2]

*SHIZUKA moves to-
wards the Orchestra,
sits down facing the
Flute-player and puts
on a tall gold cap.*

BENKEI — Here is an *eboshi*. Pray put it on.

6

SHIZUKA — I have no heart to dance

CHORUS — Because I feel ashamed to wave my sleeves.

---

[1] Quoted from a poem by Fujiwara-no-Kintō contained in the *Senzaishū*.

[2] Chinese poem from the *Wakan Rōeishū* by Ono-no-Takamura, the best poet in eighth century Japan,
who was equally skilled in the composition of Japanese and Chinese verse. The lines quoted were
written when he was banished to the islands of Oki in the Japan Sea as a punishment for disobeying
Government orders.

SHIZUKA *rises and performs an* iroe *dance.*

SHIZUKA	When Duke Tōshu, so goes the story,[1]
sashi	Followed King Kōsen to Mount Kwaikei,
CHORUS	Many a clever strategem did he there devise[2]

Until at last he crushed the King of Go
And Kōsen could have his revenge.

SHIZUKA *dances while the following lines are chanted.*

kuse When by his aid Kōsen had regained his realm

And wiped away the shame of Kwaikei,

As minister at Kōsen's court,

Duke Tōshu could have wielded boundless power,

And gained highest honours and vast possessions.

Yet, since obedient to Heaven's decree

" The wise man should retire

When fame is reached and great deeds done,"[3]

Rowing a boat on the Five Lakes[4]

He found contentment among mists and waters.

---

[1] T'ao Chu-kung (陶朱公), chief councillor to King Kōsen (Kou-chien ; 勾踐) of Yueh (越) in South China (fifth century B.C.). A hereditary feud exists between Yueh and the neighbouring kingdom of Go (Wu ; 吳) ruled by Fusa (Fu Ch'a ; 夫差). In a pitched battle fought at the foot of Mt. Kwaikei (K'uai-chi ; 會稽) King Kou-chien suffered a crushing defeat and life was spared only on condition that his kingdom should become a vassal state of Wu. For the next twenty years, at the advice of his minister T'ao Chu-kung, Kou-chien endured every kind of humiliation in his attempts to conciliate the King of Wu. At the same time he never for a moment lost sight of his secret plan to revenge himself and regain his kingdom. Finally he successfully invaded the kingdom of Wu, killed his old enemy, and annexed his territories.

[2] Inaccurate statement, as indicated in the preceding note.

[3] Quoted from Lao-tse (老子): " Gold and gems may fill one's hall, but they cannot be possessed for long ; if anyone becomes proud of his wealth and honours, he will soon run into misfortune. It is in accordance with Heaven's decree to go into retirement when one has attained success and fame.

[4] Another name for T'ai-hu (太湖), a lake in the province of Chiang-su (江蘇).

SHIZUKA	Of such examples history tells.
CHORUS	Leaving the glorious Miyako,
	If you seek safety o'er the western waves,
	There to plead your innocence,
	Yoritomo will at last towards you incline
	As willows bow before the breeze.
	How can brothers' love,
	Close-knit as branches of a willow-tree,
	Decay and cease?
	" Have but faith in me—

SHIZUKA *performs a* chū-no-mai *dance.*

SHIZUKA	Have but faith in me,
	Ye, who are like moxa-weeds on Shimeji Moor,
CHORUS	While in this world I dwell ! "[1]
SHIZUKA	If this great vow lie not,
CHORUS	If this great vow lie not,

Turns towards BENKEI.

	My lord will prosper in the world again.
	Now must his boat set forth,
	The rowers slip the moorings, crying ' Make haste,'
	The rowers slip the moorings, crying ' Make haste ! '
	Thus urged, the Hōgan leaves his lodging;
SHIZUKA	Shizuka sobbing
CHORUS	Lays aside her robe and cap ;
	Choking with tears she takes her leave ;
	O heart-rending sight,
	O heart-rending sight !

The HŌGAN *rises from the stool and takes two or three steps forward.*

SHIZUKA *removes her cap.*
The HŌGAN *follows* SHIZUKA *with his eyes as she weeping leaves the stage, then seats himself again on the stool.*

---

[1] See *Tamura*, p. 30, note 1.

PART TWO

1

BOATMAN　Lady Shizuka's sorrow at parting from her lord has made me cry, too.　But he's right not to take her with him overseas, so as to stop people's tongues wagging.　Now then, instead of muttering to myself, I should be informing Reverend Musashi that the boat is ready for Lord Hōgan.　Please your honour, I too was moved to tears by the sight of Lady Shizuka's distress at having to leave.　What does your reverence think?

Moves forward to the Shite *Pillar.*

Goes and sits on the floor in front of BENKEI.

BENKEI　I too have shed tears.　But our lord is quite right not to take her with him overseas, since he is afraid of evil tongues.　I think he has done well, don't you?

BOATMAN　Yes, well, very well!

BENKEI　Have you made ready the boat as I ordered?

BOATMAN　Yes, I have.　I have made ready a swift boat.　I can put out to sea at any time.

BENKEI　Then we shall be starting very shortly.

BOATMAN　Very well, your reverence.

Returns to the Kyō-gen *Seat.*

2

BENKEI　I can well imagine how Lady Shizuka is feeling.　But we must now put out to sea.

Rises

FIRST RETAINER　Musashi, I must speak with you.

BENKEI　What is the matter?

FIRST RETAINER　The sea is getting rough, so it is his lordship's will to stop here for to-day.

176

BENKEI   What? Has his lordship decided to stop?

FIRST RETAINER

    Yes, that's a fact.

BENKEI   I suspect his lordship is unwilling to part from Shizuka and therefore wishes to put off his departure. When you think of it, such a decision can only mean that his luck has run out. Once,[1] while he was embarking at Watanabe[2] and Fukushima,[3] it was blowing a gale. Still he ordered the boats to put out to sea and destroyed the Heike forces. We should do the same now,
    And put our boat to sea without delay.

FIRST RETAINER

    You are right.

    Enemies lurk everywhere!

BENKEI   The crew are noisy as the evening waves.

CHORUS   *Eiya, eiya*, they cry as they push out the boat

    Upon the darkling sea.

BOATMAN   All aboard!

The BOATMAN *hurries into the Mirror Room, bringing out a framework boat which he sets in front of the Waki Seat, with the bows facing the audience. Stepping into it, he stands at the stern. The* HŌGAN *gets into the boat and sits on a stool in the bows.* BENKEI *sits next to him while the* RETAINERS *sit as if they were in a boat.*

3

BOATMAN   Come, let us get under way. *Ei, ei ei. Ei, ei.* Your reverence, it is a matter for congratulation that the weather should be unusually fine for his lordship's departure.

Moves a bamboo pole back and forth as if rowing.

BENKEI   Yes, it is indeed unusually fine. I am well pleased.

BOATMAN   And I have chosen my best rowers for my lord. What do you think of them, your reverence?

[1] I.e. 1185. See p. 169, note 2.

[2,3] Both places are now part of the city of Osaka.

BENKEI   I am well pleased with your fine crew.

BOATMAN   I am glad they satisfy you. *Ei, ei, ei.* Reverend sir, I have a favour to ask of you.

BENKEI   What is it?

BOATMAN   Nothing very important. My lord goes down to the Westland because of his estrangement from Yoritomo, but since he is his brother, they should be reconciled soon, and there is no doubt his lordship will return to Miyako. In that case will you kindly put in a good word for me with his lordship so that I may be made controller of shipping for the western seas?

BENKEI   That is a reasonable request for you to make. My lord will surely come into his own again and I will then see to it that you are appointed controller of shipping in the western seas.

BOATMAN   I am very grateful to your reverence. When a lord is in need, his men are ready to make all kinds of promises, but once the need is over, they are liable to forget them. I hope you will not forget.

BENKEI   No, Musashi never forgets!

BOATMAN   Then since Reverend Musashi says so, my wish is as good as fulfilled. However, people say it is best to make assurance doubly sure, so please keep it in mind. *Ei, ei, ei.*

Looks towards the Metsuke Pillar.

How strange! See that nasty-looking cloud, which has appeared over Mount Muko.[1] I had not noticed it before; that always means wind. I don't want wind to-day. *Ei, ei.* Clouds are rolling up fast, one after another; the wind has changed. The sea has turned rough.

[1] Mountain outside Kobe, now called Rokkō.

Ho, you rowers, do your best. *Ei, ei, ei.* So *Slips his right arm* long as I am at the helm, however hard it may *out of his outer-kimono* blow, the boat will hold its course in any sea. *sleeve.* Never worry. *Ei, ei, ei.* A towering wave comes surging towards us. *Rya, rya, rya, rya. Wave, wave, wave. Shikare, shikare, shikare, shikare. Shih, shih, shih, shih. Ei, ei, ei.* You may think we are making a lot of noise, but waves are obedient and if we scold them they quiet down. *Looks towards the* *Ei, ei, ei.* *Waki* Seat.

There, a huge wave is rising again. *Wave,* *Draws a wide arc* *wave, wave. Rya, rya, rya. Shikare, shikare, shi-* *with his pole to sym-* *kare, shikare. Shih, shih, shih, shih. Ei, ei, ei.*

BENKEI   Woe is me! The wind has changed. With the wind blowing from Mount Muko and over the Peak of Yuzuriha,[1] there is no hope of getting our boat to shore. You all, from the bottom of your heart pray to gods and buddhas!

FIRST RETAINER

    Musashi, this boat is possessed by an evil spiri .

BENKEI   Please keep quiet. Such things should not be mentioned on board ship.

BOATMAN Ever since he came aboard, I knew that man would say something unlucky. Now, at last, he has come out with dreadful words. You mustn't speak of such things on an ill-omened boat.

BENKEI   Come, come, he knows nothing about ships. Please forgive him for my sake.

BOATMAN If you risk, reverend sir, I'll say no more about it. But it was too bad of him to say

1 Mountain on Awaji Island in the Inland Sea.

179

such a thing. *Ei, ei, ei.* Again another towering wave comes surging towards us. *Rya, rya,
rya. Wave, wave, wave. Shikare, shikare, shikare.
Shih, shih, shih, shih. Ei, ei, ei.*

4

BENKEI   O marvel!
            As I scan the sea,   *Rises and looks*
            The chieftains who perished in the West   *towards the Curtain.*
            Rise from the waves.
      Taking advantage of our plight it is reasonable
they should appear to wreak their vengeance
on us.

HŌGAN   Benkei!

BENKEI   At your service, my lord.

HŌGAN   We need not be afraid. What harm could
those evil spirits do us?
            The Heike clan
            Defying gods and buddhas
            Committed untold sins and crimes
            And were by Heaven chastised
            And drowned beneath the waves,—

CHORUS   I see now the erstwhile emperor and his
            lords
            Rising in swarms out of the sea.

5

While the entrance music haya-fue *is being played,*
the GHOST *of Tomomori enters with a halbert on
his shoulder and stops at the* Shite *Seat and rests
the butt of his halbert on the stage. He wears a*

180

crescent-shaped mask, flowing black-hair wig, and golden horns, heavy silk kimono, gold-brocade robe, divided skirt and sword.

TOMOMORI

Behold me!
I am the ghost of Taira-no-Tomomori,
Scion of the Emperor Kammu,
In the ninth generation.
Hail, Yoshitsune!
I have come

Addresses the Hō-GAN who puts his hand to his sword.

Guided by your oarsmen's voices,

The GHOST moves towards the front of the stage.

CHORUS

As your boat cleaves
The waters of Daimotsu Bay,
As your boat cleaves
The waters of Daimotsu Bay.

TOMOMORI

I, Tomomori,

CHORUS

Will drag down Yoshitsune
Under the waves beneath which I sank.
Grasping his halbert,
He whirls it round him like a flail,
Churning up the waves
And belching forth noisome vapours.
Dizzy-eyed and mind distraught,
None know where they are.

The GHOST dances while the following lines are chanted.

The GHOST dances a hataraki *dance.*

6

HŌGAN

But Yoshitsune, undismayed,

CHORUS

But Yoshitsune, undismayed,
Draws his sword;
As if he were a man
He challenges him to combat.

The HŌGAN draws his sword.

The HŌGAN and the GHOST fight.

181

Then they engage, but Benkei
    thrusts between, saying:
" Swords are of no avail,"
And rubs the beads between
    his hands.

From the east he invokes
    Gozanze Myōō,[1]
From the south Gundari Yasha Myōō,
From the west Dai Itoku Myōō,

From the north Kongō Yasha Myōō,
And in the centre Fudō Myōō
And calls upon that Great King

To bind the evil spirits with his sacred
    rope.

The GHOST *re-
treats to the Third Pine,
then throwing away his
halbert and drawing
his sword, he again
moves towards the*
HŌGAN.

As one by one they all fall back,
Benkei aids the rowers
To speed his master's boat
And bring it safe to shore.
The still-pursuing spirits are put to flight
By Benkei's prayers;
Then on the tide they drift away
Leaving no trace upon the foaming waves.

The GHOST *returns
to the Third Pine and
stamps twice.*

[1] *Myōō* (Divya raja) are incarnations of Buddha as the ' Body of Law.' They assume fierce and terrifying forms in order to quell men of a stubborn evil nature. The five most powerful of these kings are especially venerated by the Japanese sect of ' mountain ascetics.' Four are enthroned in each of the four quarters, while the fifth, i.e. Fudō (Acalanatha), occupies the centre. Fudō is represented holding in his right hand a sword symbolizing widsom and in his left a rope symbolizing mercy, and is surrounded by flames, which have a virtue of consuming all evil thoughts and passions.

INDEX

J

Jakushō, 43n
Ji sect, 40n
jidori, xiv, 6, 24 and *passim*
Jikkinshō, 109n, 111
Jingū, Empress, 8n
Jishu Gongen (Land-Owner Deity), 22n, 25n, 28 and *passim* in *Tamura*
jiura, xii
jo, xvi, 22
Jōdo-kyō, 40n, 43n, 97n
jo-ha-kyū principle, xvi
John, St., 98n
jo-no-mai, xv, 77, 78, 88, 93, 104, 123, 127, 140
Juei era, 70
Jūrō Motomasa, 146

K

kachi-shura (victory Asura), 21
kagami-ita (large wooden panel), xii
kagami-no-ma (mirror room), xii
Kajiwara-no-Kagetoki, 168n
kake-kotoba (pivot-word), xvii
kakemono, 4
kakeri, xv, 21, 35, 59, 145, 150
kake-suō robe (*kake-suō*), 61, 148
Kamakura, 163n, 164n, 168n
Kamakura government, 163n, 164n
kami-asobi, 4
kami-mai, xv, 16
kami-mai-mono, 3
Kami Noh, xvi
Kammu, Emperor, 33n, 181
Kamo, river, 87
Kantan' mask, ' man of, xvi, 15
karukaya (*Themeda triandria*), 141
Kasumi-ga-seki, 80n, see Barrier of Mists
katari, xiv, 26, 40, 51, 153
Katsura, river, 114n
kazura-mono (female-wig piece), xvi, 77, 93, 109, 127
kenjo, xii
Ki-no-Aritsune's daughter, 93, 94, 95 and *passim* in *Izutsu*

Ki-no-Tomo-o, 35n
Ki-no-Tsurayuki, 82n, 86
Ki-no-Yoshimochi, 86n
kiri, xiv
Kiri Noh (programme-concluding play), xvi, 163
kirido-guchi (sliding door), xii
Kisen, Monk, 93n
Kiso Mountains, 39n
Kiso, Lord, 39, 51, 54
Kiso Yoshinaka, 39n, 164n
Kita, xvii
Kita-Shirakawa, 150, 154
Kiyomizu (pure water), 22n, 27n, 30
Kiyomizu-dera, 22, 28n, 32, see Seisui-ji Temple
Kiyomizu Kwannon, 30n
Kiyomori, 59n, 164n, 165n, see Taira-no-Kiyomori
Kiyotsune, 59, 60, 61, and *passim* in *Kiyotsune*
Kiyotsune's wife, 59, 60, 61 and *passim* in *Kiyotsune*
Kōbun-boku, 81
Kōfuku-ji, 95n
Kojidan, 111
Kojiki, xvii
kokata (boy actor), xiii, 147, 165, 167
kōken, xiii
Kokinshū, 3, 7n, 9, and *passim*
Komparu, xvii
Komparu Zenchiku, 128
Kongō, xvii
Kongō Yasha Myōō, 182
Konjaku Monogatari, xvii, 22
Kōsen (Kou-chien), King, 174
Koshikibu, Lady, 77n.
Koshima Temple, 27
kotoba, xiv
Kotsu, river, 27
Kou-chien, 174n, see Kōsen
K'uai-chi, 54n, 174n, see Kwaikei
Kumano, 28n
Kunaikyō, Lady, 149n
kuri, xiv, 11, 51, 86, 100, 139

INDEX

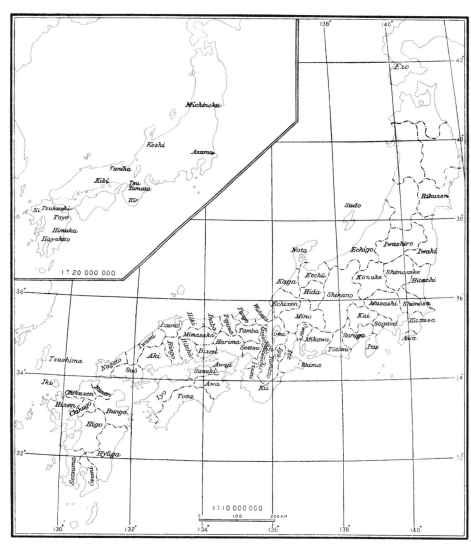

1:20 000 000

Ezo

138°   140°

42°

Michinoku

Koshi   Azuma   40°

Tariha   Rikuzen
Kibi   Tsu
        Yamato   Sado
        Ki
Hi Tsukushi   Echigo   Iwashiro
    Toyo   Noto   Iwaki
    Himuka   Kōzuke Shimozuke   38°
    Hayahito   Etchū Kaga   Hitachi
                            Hida   Shinano
36°   Echizen   Musashi Shimōsa   36°
                Hōki   Mino Kai Sagami Kazusa
            Izumo Inaba Tajima Tamba Ōmi Mikawa Suruga Awa
        Iwami   Mimasaka   Settsu Ise Tōtōmi Izu
    Tsushima Bingo Bitchū Bizen Harima Iga Owari Shima
        Aki   Yamato
34° Nagato Suō Sanuki Awaji   34°
    Iki   Awa Kii
        Iyo Tosa
    Chikuzen Buzen
Hizen Chikugo Bungo
        Higo
32°   Hyūga   32°

    Satsuma
        Ōsumi

1:10 000 000
0   100   200 KM
134°   136°   138°   140°
130°   132°

JAPAN in PROVINCES